WORTHtheWAIT

D1531706

WORTHtheWAIT

TIM STAFFORD

A DIVISION OF CTi
CampusLife | TYNDALE HOUSE
BOOKS | PUBLISHERS, INC.
WHEATON, ILLINOIS

All Scripture quotations are from *The Holy Bible,* New International Version, copyright 1978 by the New York International Bible Society.

First printing, April 1988

Library of Congress Catalog Card Number 88-50101
ISBN 0-8423-8375-1
Copyright 1988 by Campus Life Books, a division of CTi
All rights reserved
Printed in the United States of America

CONTENTS

CHAPTER ONE

WHY IT'S HARD TO WAIT

Why would God create all this sexual energy in me and never allow me to release it?

That's the question Paul, a nineteen-year-old guy from North Carolina, asked me. It's an excellent question. Sex is not an abstract subject we can discuss like the composition of the moon. It's a living presence, or pressure, inside each one of us.

Of course, Paul overstated what God asks him to do. God doesn't ask him *never* to release his sexual energy. God asks him to save the ultimate expression of sex—intercourse—until he's married. But, intercourse is not the only way to release sexual energy. And "until you're married" is certainly not "never."

However, Paul wasn't overstating anything when he spoke of "all this sexual energy in me." With such tremendous stirrings inside, waiting for marriage can seem like "never."

It is hard to wait. Of course, many people don't care to try. But even for those who want to, waiting for marriage is hard. At nineteen, Paul speaks for a lot of other people.

Why is sex so attractive? Why do people think of it so much? Why does a single glimpse of a good-looking somebody set off an explosion in your brain?

And why does sex sweep people into doing things they vowed they never would? Why do they get carried away? Why does sex seem so much more powerful than our so-called willpower? How come it throws common sense out the window?

WHO PUT THE POWER INSIDE?

There is no mystery to these questions. If you must blame someone for the power of sex, you can blame God. He made you sexually alive. He put the power there. But while you're blaming him, give God some credit, too. What would life be like without sex?

I remember when an extra room was being built onto our house. First the contractor laid the foundation. Then he put up the frame. That's when the electrician came and wove a network of wires in and out of that wooden skeleton. Compared to the beams, the wires weren't very noticeable. Later on when the walls were covered with sheetrock, siding, insulation, and paint, I couldn't even see them except in a few spots where they protruded.

One day when the room was ready for living, the electric company came and connected that network into the main source of power. Suddenly those wires became extremely significant. I couldn't see any change; the wires were still hidden. But then that room became good for more than keeping the rain out. I could do things I couldn't before. I could plug in my stereo and listen to the Beatles. I could run my computer. I could stay up late reading Dickens.

I could also electrocute myself if I did something stupid.

Sexuality is something like that. Biologically, your potential was wired in at birth. You have the proper organs. You have a male or female mix of hormones. That's good. God said so. When he had finished with the whole creation, topping it off with male and female human beings, he stepped back and observed that it was "very good." That includes your sexuality.

To most people, though, sexuality doesn't seem that significant until puberty. That's when their wiring gets hooked into power. Suddenly sexuality becomes an active potential. Males and females become charged particles, ready to bond. That's good, too, because God made them, and he knew what he was doing.

WHY YOU WANT TO GET INTO ACTION

"Every time I hear his voice, I get this funny feeling inside." A girl wrote that describing her boyfriend, but the same idea could have been expressed by a guy.

You begin to feel, at puberty, that the opposite sex is more than something to wonder about. If you're a guy, you want a girl for your own. If you're a girl, you want a guy. It's a strong and thrilling (sometimes even frightening) urge to bond.

Physically, you want to touch: to hold hands, to kiss, ultimately to make love. Psychologically you want to touch also: to probe the depths of a personality, to love and be loved, to expose your thoughts and your fears, to be open and transparent.

With this longing comes fear: *Will I ever love? Will I ever be loved? Am I wired right? Will I find the person I dream of? Or will I be left behind?*

God made you with sexual longings. Let's even go so far as to say this: he made you in such a way that it's hard to wait. Call it a challenge, flung down by the Creator God: "I'll give you this amazing potential. But know in advance: it is not easy to master. It will test you to your limits."

If it's a challenge, it is also a compliment. God challenges us because he believes we can live up to the challenge.

There's nothing immoral or second-rate in dreaming about the fulfillment of your sexuality. Just make sure you dream the whole dream.

Like so many people, I intended to wait until after marriage to have sex. But then I met this one particular guy who became very special to me. We dated each other for a year and a half, and for the first twelve months I resisted all of the physical "pressure" he put on me. I explained again and again that I wanted to wait, but eventually I gave in. I can make all kinds of excuses for what happened—I was having a very hard time accepting my parents' divorce, and I felt very lonely—but that doesn't change the facts. Of course, at that time we "loved" each other and were planning marriage, and I didn't think it really mattered too much.

I'm sure you can guess the outcome. Not very long after we made love, he decided he didn't "love" me anymore—then we broke up. The guilt and hurt that I experienced lasted nine months. During those months I had to talk to many understanding friends to try to learn to forgive myself and to get over caring for him so much. But even now I still experience a twinge of pain that will never completely go away.

It's a hard way to learn the truth. I had a lot of good advice that I never bothered to listen to. I just never thought my situation would end that way. Now I know all too well that once you start getting physical, finding a "good stopping place" before going all the way is almost impossible. I've learned, too, that at age seventeen I really didn't know anything at all about the true, lasting love that comes from a deep commitment. Now, at eighteen, I still can't comprehend the perfect love that will come in marriage.

I know many people my age have heard the same advice again and again, but maybe my experience will influence someone not to be sexually involved before marriage. I didn't listen, but now I know: the pain of ending a relationship tied up with sex is much worse than ending one without it. Sex is meant to bind two people together forever. I feel like I've lost a part of me to him that will never return and can never be replaced. ▬

WHAT COULD GO WRONG?

What's the worst thing that could happen to you sexually? Some people imagine disaster as missing out on sex and being a monk all their life.

From God's perspective, however, sexual disaster is different. He wants more than the mere physical performance of the sex act for you. He's concerned that you might fail to get all the joy and pleasure he intended when he gave you this powerful drive.

Most people worry about missing out on the good things promised by their sexual drive, but they usually concentrate on relatively insignificant problems. They fear being rejected because they have acne or a long nose, or because they are too shy or aren't popular. They fear missing the person they're meant to bond with—that they'll pass like legendary ships in the night.

I hear this all the time in the letters people write me for my column in *Campus Life* magazine: "I'm seventeen years old and my friends tell me I'm quite attractive. But I don't have a boyfriend. I've never had a boyfriend. *Can you tell me what I'm doing wrong?*" This girl, like many others, fears some hidden factor is jinxing her. Her life is being ruined by something she doesn't even know about.

Or, "I met this girl at summer camp, and we got really close. Now that camp's over she's four-hundred miles away. I hardly ever get to see her and we're drifting apart. I know there are lots of fish in the sea, but *what if she's the one for me?*" Guys like this fear they might drift past their once-in-a-lifetime chance for lasting love—and regret it forever.

But that's not how people generally miss out on sexual fulfillment. People miss out because they settle for pieces of the dream. They're so anxious not to miss out on love that they grab the first chance they get.

It's like me when I'm hungry. I look in the refrigerator and check out the possibilities, but instead of preparing a decent meal I grab something handy—usually junk—and start munching on it. Pretty soon I'm not hungry. But I'm not really satisfied either.

What do you really long for? When a glance from a handsome hunk of personality knocks you sideways, what is the basic longing behind that dizziness you feel? That's an important question because it will determine what you're willing to settle for.

Some people settle for short-term goals: *What I want, really want, is for Rick to ask me out.* Of course, no one is really satisfied with just a date; a person soon wants more. But a short-termer sets goals one day at a time. First, a date with that wonderful person she's been watching. Then, the title deed known as *going together.* That means belongs to her. What then? Usually, a new target. Forget about Rick. *What I want, really want, is for Stefan to ask me out.*

People with short-term goals usually end up with short-term relationships. Even the few that last long-term are usually immature. The relationship doesn't grow toward anything; it's just stuck in the "I've-got-you-and-I'll-never-let-you-go" phase. That doesn't satisfy your deepest desires.

Let's Get Physical

Other people settle for the purely physical side of the dream. *What I want, really want, is her body.* There's a powerful payoff: Sex just plain feels great. Your body wants this pleasure and drives you toward it.

You can easily think of sex as a physical thing. Most people do at times. But that's not really all you want either.

If sex were just body-desire, pornography would be admirable. It's the purest form of impersonal sex. True, you don't get a body—just a picture of a body. But you don't get any personal complications either. No nasty breakups. No disappointments. None of the endless problems you get with real people. Just the sheer, fascinating, heart-thumping excitement of seeing the unthinkable undressed and looking only at you— so willing, so eager. Sex is never so perfect as when you're alone with your fantasies (or other people's).

Those who prefer real bodies to imaginary partners can achieve almost the same effect. They can call it "no-promises sex," and keep it untangled by commitments. It seems to be a good deal for both people: You give me my pleasure, I'll give you yours. Or if we're not exchanging sexual pleasure in a straight trade, we can barter. You give me the security of having a girlfriend every weekend, I'll make sure you end the evening satisfied. You take me out to dinner, I'll put out. And when we've gotten what we want out of this relationship, long term or short, you go your way and I'll go mine.

Sexual adventurers who treat sex as a gourmet experience seem to be everywhere. They talk a lot, so you notice them more. But the percentage of people who are satisfied with "just physical" sex is really quite low. Many of them, after playboying around for a few years, decide to settle down. It has been said, "It's hard to keep sex just plain fun." Great as sex feels, the physical sensations are over in a few minutes. That can leave you feeling sad and empty if there's nothing lasting behind the physical sensations—no real caring, no real love. You want something more, something more personal. You're a person, not a pleasure machine. You want intimacy, not just sex. You want lasting love.

But that doesn't mean that you'll be satisfied with just moonlit evenings, good-night kisses and valentines either. Time was when the whole approach to teenage love was dating and romance. Sex—the physical side—went practically unmentioned. But not unthought. Or even unexperienced. We're not wired for just romance either.

We want body plus personality, sex *and* love. We dream of bonding flesh and soul with another person forever. And that's the dream we were made to dream. That's why we want to get into action. That's why it's so hard to wait. God made us to desire emotional, spiritual, and physical completion—and he gave us marriage as the place for two people to find that completion.

Yet how easily we settle for pieces of the dream—and how quickly our dreams can fall to pieces.

CHAPTER TWO

THE PRESSURES OF A MODERN SOCIETY

How do you have a relationship God's way when the examples we have are the shallow TV relationships?

The pressures we feel aren't all God's doing. Some are due to our environment.

I've compared sexuality to electrical wiring: it seems insignificant until the power goes on. But there's another factor: the number of appliances available to plug in.

If you check an old house that was wired before 1950, you'll find its original equipment included only one or two electrical outlets per room. People who live in such houses nowadays either rewire them or run yards of extension cord under rugs and around corners, making a real fire hazard.

Why did they build houses with so few outlets? It wasn't that it cost so much to put in a few more. The reason was that nobody needed more outlets. Nobody had that many appliances to plug in. A family had a radio, a fan, a few lamps, a refrigerator. No TV. No VCR. No freezer. No microwave. No blender. No coffeemaker. No electric can opener. No curling iron. No computer. No air conditioner. No battery recharger. Consequently, families in the fifties used less electricity. The potential was there in terms of power, but how much of that power got used depended on what nifty appliances society made available.

So it is with sexuality. The wiring is standard equipment on every model. The power is there. But society greatly influences what you're tempted to plug into it.

First off, society controls what's possible. In a strict Muslim country, for instance, society says a guy will be lucky to see the color of his beloved's eyes before the honeymoon. In America today, however, everything imaginable is within reach. There's plenty of privacy and freedom for a couple of well-wired kids to do whatever they please. Parents may tell you "Don't!" but they can't control you.

Second, society tells what to expect. If everybody in my school has a VCR, I'm going to consider myself deprived if I don't. If everybody in my school sleeps together by the third date (or claims to), that will greatly influence my expectations of what my third date may be like.

And what expectations does American society set for sex? There are conflicting messages. What you hear in church or at home may be quite conservative. Out in the big wide world, however, the message is mostly, "Sex is inevitable."

On TV morality is a joke. Everybody is on the make. It's sometimes a big *Wow* (as in, "Wow, can you believe they're saying that on TV?"), or sometimes a Noble Quest for Fulfillment between two people who are so passionately in love they can't help themselves. More and more it's just the way things are: two attractive people are going to go to bed together. Sex is as normal as plugging in a blender.

According to one recent study, the average TV-watching American gets treated to 9,230 scenes depicting sexual intercourse, sexual comments, or innuendo each year. Another study estimated that for every time TV suggests sex between married people, it portrays six sexual encounters between unmarried people.

A SLIGHT BACKING OFF

Just lately, with the fear of AIDS all around, there has been some backing away from this. A few shows promote family values. Even in those that don't a strange note of responsibility occasionally will enter in. A heated-up couple in a teledrama will actually stop short of going all the way because they don't have a condom to protect themselves. Or a kid may explain to his girlfriend that he doesn't feel ready for sex and he wants to wait until he's sure.

This isn't really a change in the underlying message. It's just a refinement. It's the equivalent of that timeless scared-parent farewell as a kid goes out on a date: "Be careful!" There's no doubt that, whatever happens in today's teledrama episode, sex remains inevitable in a future episode. Next week they'll bring a condom with them. Next week the kid won't be so scared—he'll have gotten used to the idea, he'll be more "mature."

Once in a while you see a terribly serious documentary on TV informing us of the plague of teenage pregnancies, or the plight of the American family, or AIDS. Somebody may be given thirty seconds to suggest that the root of the problem is our view of what's right and wrong in sexual behavior. By and large, though, this message gets drowned out by the assumption that everybody is, or soon will be, sexually active. The assumption is that people will go to bed together regardless of the consequences, and society will just have to provide the condoms, or the medical facilities, or the abortions, or whatever is required to clean up the mess it caused.

Someone may add, "You teenagers should probably wait until you're sixteen or eighteen." That's another parents' adage: "You're not old enough. Wait until you're an adult—then it'll be OK. Wait until you're responsible—like me."

I never met a kid who believed that what's wrong at fifteen becomes right at twenty-five. That's too arbitrary. Especially when he's in love.

WHAT ABOUT MY MOM?

Even the message of "wait until you're older" is getting preached less and less. Adults usually would rather their kids not be sexually involved, but they find it hard to preach what they don't practice. Here's what one girl wrote to me:

> I am a fifteen-year-old girl who has a problem not many of my friends understand. My mom and her boyfriend started dating about three years ago. We soon started spending the night at his house. This didn't bother me because my mom and I slept in the front bedroom. But then they started sleeping together. This also didn't bother me much, until one night I went back there to ask my mother something and her boyfriend came out of the bathroom with his underwear on (and just his underwear). Then I soon caught them having sex.

Not so long ago, *mothers* wrote letters like that about their *daughters*. But now, millions of kids whose parents are divorced have the tables turned. They see their parents getting involved in immorality. They see their parents shattered and hardened by the breakups and disappointments that inevitably follow. Naturally, these parents are not giving their children much encouragement to wait for marriage.

Or consider the way Kathryn Burkhart, in the book *Growing into Love,* put her prescription for teenage morality: "It seems to me that adolescents of all ages should be encouraged to have foreplay and to defer intercourse until they are extremely comfortable in their own bodies and very much at ease about themselves and their sexual partners. Teenagers should think about their own requirements for sexual intimacy and have great respect for their own feelings and values."

Unfortunately that's as strong as morality gets in much of our society. How it will affect behavior in the back bedroom I will leave you to guess. I can just hear Burkhart's morality applied: "Molly, are you comfortable in your body?" "Uh-huh." "Do you feel at ease with yourself and with me?" "Oh, yeah!" "Do you have great respect for your own feelings and values?" "You bet!" Two guesses how that conversation ends.

SEX FOR PROFIT

Movies don't even include this kind of light-handed morality. In movies, sex is a great deal more inevitable than it is in life. The reason is simple: sex sells. Apparently movie producers have concluded that you can't have a successful movie without some sex involved. They have a rating system that enables you to guess just what will be displayed. PG: a few flashes of skin, romantic music, R: breasts, lots of skin, extended lovemaking. X: it's probably violent. But regardless of what skin gets shown, sex is nearly always shown, whatever the rating. Boy meets girl. Boy goes to bed with girl. The mystery is no longer like the old Doris Day movies: will she or won't she? The only mystery is when and how? And also, how come nobody gets pregnant? (Unfortunately, millions of teenagers *do* get pregnant each year. But only in real life. Never in the movies.)

Music is, in some ways, less explicit. That's because musical lyrics usually leave a lot to your imagination. However, it's no longer a guessing game to figure out the "dirty" lyrics to songs. Nobody has to sneak stuff in any more. It's out front. Music has long been romantic and preoccupied with love. Nowadays it's assumed: sex goes with the package.

There's another message-sender you may not think about: advertising. Almost every ad you see—in magazines, on TV, or on billboards—

is bathed in sexual messages. Beautiful bodies; alluring looks; glistening skin, eyes, hair. They get your attention, don't they? Surely advertising contributes to the fundamental assumption that comes through on TV, in music, in movies, in magazines—that sex is inevitable. Only the physically ugly or the psychologically disturbed—losers all the way—fail to make it.

Everywhere you turn it's the same. Dr. Ruth, even Dear Abby, assume that sex is inevitable for properly wired people. They'll even come out and say it: "Once upon a time people could believe that sex was a no-no. But we're not living in the dark ages. In the twentieth century, we can't bury our heads in the sand and pretend that people aren't going to have sex. It's inevitable."

They don't mention that for most of the history of the world (and even today in many countries) sex outside marriage was not inevitable. People were wired just the same as we are. But in their minds, *marriage* was inevitable. Ordinary, healthy, highly sexed people waited for marriage. And they believed it was worth the wait.

Q: I realize that the Bible considers sex to be for marriage only. But in those times people were married at twelve, thirteen, fourteen. That was when their bodies were just developing. They didn't have any "urges" or "needs" physically to be dealt with.

I am a nineteen-year-old virgin. Guys, no matter who they are (I've tried all types—even guys from church), want to have sexual relations. They want to have a "deeper" relationship with me. They say it brings two people closer together.

Financially, socially, two young people can't get married today. They won't be able to survive out in this world. But their bodies have been ready since they were thirteen or fourteen. It was fine back when the Bible was written, but what about now? Did God keep this in mind? Is he making it more difficult for a reason? It's not fair that we were born in this time.

I am a Christian to the end. It is so hard each time I let a guy go because we can't go further in our relationship. Even if we have God as a common factor. I can handle it, but they can't. They hurt me more in this type of relationship than if we had sex and left one another afterwards.

None of my friends understand why I'm holding out. They say times have changed. I don't know. Help me out, please.

A: You're right about the age of marriage in biblical times. People did usually marry young. (They also lived with their parents for the rest of their lives. That side of the arrangement is less appealing, I'd say.)

And I agree with you: waiting longer makes it tough. You have to put off your sexual urges for a very long time. I know it's hard: I did it. It must be doubly hard when you're surrounded by people who don't share your values.

But the guys you've known don't represent everybody. According to the best recent research, *Sex and the American Teenager* from Rolling Stone Press, about half of all teenagers, both male and female, stay virgins through their teenage years. I'm not denying that a lot of sexual activity goes on in high school. I know there's plenty. But there's quite a lot of determined virginity, too.

But that's not your question. You want to know whether, as times change, our sense of right and wrong should, too.

How much have times changed? You might be tempted to exaggerate the difference. Sexual purity has never come easily; if all urges and desires had been neatly dealt with by teenage marriages, there would have been no reason for the Bible to warn against sex outside marriage. Sexual impulses are always hard to contain.

But when we're comparing our situation to theirs, why limit it to just sex? Maybe sexual purity is harder now; but some commands must be easier. What about the commands not to steal or covet? In biblical times people lived one rainy season away from starvation. They had few possessions; a second set of clothes was a luxury. Compared to us, don't you think they found it harder not to steal or covet? They could hardly imagine how people like us could be greedy and have a high rate of burglary.

What I'm saying is this: Every era has its unique difficulties. Not only that, but every stage of life has its unique difficulties. My mother used to tell me that the young are tempted by sex, the middle-aged by greed, and the old by grumbling. Do you think it's fair that many old people have to maintain thankful hearts despite feeling rotten every morning? On the other hand, they may feel less intense sexual urges. Does that make it easier for them to be faithful Christians? Not necessarily. Your temptations change—your need for God's help doesn't.

You have a choice. You can concentrate on the difficulties life throws at you, or you can concentrate on the wonderful strength that God gives you to face them. He has said, clearly enough, that no one faces temptation too big to beat: "No temptation has seized you except what is common to man. And God is faithful; he will not let you be tempted beyond what you can bear. But when you are tempted, he will also provide a way out so that you can stand up under it" (1 Corinthians 10:13).

And by the way, it may be hard to get dumped by a guy because you won't have sex, but it's better than getting dumped by a guy *after* you've had sex. I have heard from a lot of girls who would agree.

It may be harder to follow God's commands on sex than it once was, but the protection you get from obedience has not changed a bit. You don't ever have to know what it feels like to give all you've got to some-body—and then get rejected. ▰▰▰

CHAPTER THREE

PEER PRESSURE

I have been going steady with the same guy for almost two years. I love him very much and I know without a doubt that he loves me. We go to church regularly because his parents are pastors of our church, and we both share a musical ministry that glorifies God to the fullest. I have had sex with him only once, and now it's leading to oral sex. I don't feel guilty when it's happening. But a day or two later I do. When I'm with him my love for him seems to overrule any guilty feeling that I could have.

It's a known fact that the TV you watch, the movies you see, the news-papers you read, and the music you hear will have an impact on your thinking, particularly when they all carry the same message, a message that appeals to a very powerful urge that God wired into you.

But that message doesn't carry as much weight as the opinion of a few good friends. Society's message, whatever it is, has to get translated down to your level. For example: just why does everybody come to school dressed in the same kind of shoes? You see the advertisements, but what really sells you is when your friends start wearing the shoes.

Society's sexual-inevitability message gets translated into your local language this way: Your two best friends become sexually involved. One likes to tell you all about it. She embarrasses you to death with the details. The other friend considers it a private matter and even though you hint about it, she lets few details leak. Yet neither one shows any sign of regret. They're both all wrapped up in their relationships. You feel odd, left behind. You feel you don't have as much in common with your friends as you used to. You feel dumb. Not many people like to remain odd and ignorant of what's going on. Get the message?

Q: I'm writing in response to the fifteen-year-old Christian girl who wrote telling you she and her boyfriend don't feel guilty about having sex. When I was fourteen, the same thing happened. My boyfriend and I both attended a Christian high school, and we knew premarital sex was wrong, but we loved each other and felt it only deepened our relationship. Many times we tried to quit, but it never lasted, and our relationship got . . . stronger(?) Well, maybe—if stronger means his demands on me to have sex in the worst places grew, with less and less consideration of my feelings. When our relationship became rocky and he wanted to break up, I couldn't bear the thought of *my* boyfriend being shared with someone else.

Well, we stuck it out, and when I was eighteen, he nineteen, we married. We never fought or argued (the only thing we had argued over before was sex). We just lived together without guilt—but also without respect for each other's feelings. We had lost that years ago. And sex was no big deal because that sacredness was thrown out the window. Did you ever eat too much cookie dough, and when the cookies were baked, you didn't want any?

Well, with all those years of rejecting God's law of purity, after one year of marriage, my husband left me and moved in with a girl he worked with. It wasn't until then—until I sat alone, rejected, pregnant and burned by the fire I had kindled—that I finally understood why the Bible says to *wait*. How can a man (or woman) honor God by keeping a marriage covenant when he couldn't honor him (and each other) before marriage? We surely reap what we sow.

A: Thank you for sharing your experience, as dreadful as it is. Your letter is a frightening reminder that we're really not playing a game. Our lives are shaped by our choices. I hear from many people who are making choices about their sexual lives; I rarely receive such a sobering account of where those choices can lead.

Yet I can't completely agree with your last sentence. We don't have to reap what we sow, though by all that's natural we should. The Christian message is good news: Jesus reaped all the death and destruction we sow for ourselves. He died for us, so that we could escape from the normal consequences of our choices: external death and separation from God. I feel for you as you describe your sense of well-deserved desperation. I don't have any magic to make it all right. The pattern you established, which took five years to reach its conclusion, may take even longer to be made right. Yet, in God's mercy it *can* be. He loves you. He cares for you. Most important, he forgives all who seek his forgiveness. There is a new beginning. ■■■

Or, another translation of society's message: You go to a party with a friend. Sometime in the middle you notice the friend is missing. Looking around, you stumble into a back bedroom where something intimate is going on in the dark, something that definitely doesn't include you. You're shocked and embarrassed, and you back out of there like a person whose shoes have caught fire. Yet you soon notice that nobody else at the party seems surprised at what's going on. You realize you've been naive. Not many people like to be naive. Get the message?

Or, another translation: You're a girl who's finally asked out by a guy you've liked for a long time. You're nervous and excited about the event. After the movie, he asks you how you feel about sex. You explain your views about waiting for marriage. He's a really nice guy and he respects you. With surprise in his voice he says, "I certainly didn't think there were good-looking girls who thought that way any more." You realize that's not just a line—you really do seem very odd to him. Get the message?

Society's message, translated to the local level by your friends, won't force you to get into the action. Peer pressure isn't usually a gang of menacing punks yelling in chorus, "Do it! Do it!" Peer pressure comes when you notice that everybody else is doing it or thinking about doing it at the very first good opportunity. Peer pressure doesn't force you to go against your conscience. It just plants the idea and gives you a nudge in that direction—like, "There's chocolate cake on top of the refrigerator if you want any."

Your God-given, high-powered wiring will do the rest as soon as you find another charged particle to pair off with. Unless something makes you want to wait.

What could make you want to wait?

PHYSICAL DESIRE

The greatest pressure of all is related to the longing God built into your body—the longing to bond with a member of the opposite sex. That longing grows like corn in July when you begin to focus on one particular person. It's called being in love.

Here's what one person wrote:

> *I used to have a strong stand against premarital sex. I felt it was absolutely wrong. I would even advise my friends who came to me for my opinion to never have sex before marriage; it was wrong. But at the time I spoke these words I had never experienced strong love [or infatuation, which can be just as strong] with a guy. One intensely physical relationship changed that. I weakened those walls against sex I had built up all of my childhood. Now I know how weak I can get when I'm in love.*

When you're in love with someone, you can't get close enough. You want to be together every hour of every day. You get a certain tingly feeling just thinking about each other. And that specific longing for closeness leads very naturally and beautifully toward sex. Sex is the natural expression of love between a man and a woman.

A girl wrote me, "Sometimes I want to make love with him because I just feel so comfortable with him. I know he wants to also, but I'm glad that when I say stop or no he doesn't lay a guilt trip on me. But sometimes I don't want to say stop."

The Bible calls sexual intercourse "knowing" each other. There's great wisdom in that. Sex is not merely physical pleasure. It's a way of experiencing and expressing the deepest possible intimacy. When you love someone, you want all of him, body and soul. You don't want to hold back, and all your theories about how you want to hold off sex until marriage can quickly go out the window.

PUPPY LOVE

People often try to make distinctions between superficial feelings and real love. They talk about "puppy love" and "infatuation." They say, "Wait for real love." I agree that there is a difference between superficial love and deeper love. However, I don't think there is any difference in the feelings. People forget how love felt when they were younger.

A kid in the seventh grade who feels "in love" may feel it just as intensely as someone who's twenty-seven. There's not much use in suggesting he put sex on hold until he feels "real love," because puppy love feels like "real love" when you're in the middle of it.

When you feel in love with someone, it's hard to believe that sexual intimacy, which feels so good, could be a mistake. "It brought us closer together," people say. "It didn't feel dirty. It felt warm and close."

One guy wrote, "It's hard to understand why it feels so beautiful if it isn't right. It makes us feel so close, so totally amazing."

"I DON'T WANT TO LOSE YOU"

I've been dating Mark for almost seven months. I am a struggling Christian. He has no religion. I plan to stay a virgin until I'm married, but he pressures me. In the beginning we talked everything out, set the rules. Mark says he loves and respects me but just can't help himself. I get tired of pushing him off, saying no. I get tired of trying to explain to him it's not because I don't love him. I find myself giving in because I don't want to lose him, because his wants become my wants.

Love can also create sexual pressure through a partner. The girl I've quoted didn't necessarily want to express her love sexually. But her boyfriend did. And she didn't want to lose him. She wanted to make him happy. She loved him, she wanted their relationship to be good, and her sexual resistance seemed to be making it miserable. Why not just give in for the sake of the relationship? Why make such an issue out of it? Isn't love what matters?

The stereotype is that guys want sex, and girls want love, and so guys give love (or at least say, "I love you") to get sex, and girls give sex to get love. It does work that way a lot of the time, but not always. For instance:

My girlfriend has been pressuring me to have sex with her. I do not believe in premarital sex. Of course, it seems tempting because I'm only human, but I know I would feel guilty if I lost my virginity before marriage. I really love my girlfriend, but I'm afraid that if I don't give in to her needs, our relationship will end.

A lot of people go against their judgment and have sex for the sake of the relationship. That seems to matter more than a standard.

Your body drives you toward sex. Society tells you it's inevitable. And the power of love can be overwhelming.

Why should you wait?

CHAPTER FOUR

SOME GOOD REASONS TO WAIT

Some people think AIDS will do what no amount of preaching about morality could: scare people into waiting until marriage to have sex. Maybe it will, but I'm skeptical.

The facts are certainly scary: (1) If you catch AIDS, you die; (2) You can pass it through intercourse between male and female; and (3) The only absolute safeguard is keeping to just one sex partner who has had no other sex partners, for life. (Condoms, widely advertised as providing "safe sex," don't. A more accurate description would be, "less-dangerous sex.")

AIDS gets your attention like a pistol held to your head. There has never been anything quite like it. It's worth putting into context, however, by noting that AIDS is the latest in a long line of sexually-transmitted diseases (STD's). Other STD's can be incurable: herpes, particularly. Some others can be deadly. Syphilis, though it works slowly, will eventually cause brain damage, insanity, and death if it isn't treated—and for two-hundred years there was no cure.

Chlamydia is an infection you may not know you have because its initial symptoms can be so subtle. One common result of Chlamydia for both men and women is infertility. One day a girl may come to realize she is never going to have a baby and learn that the problem started with somebody so far back in her past that she can't even remember what he looks like.

Herpes is a lot more obvious: it hurts, and it looks terrible when it flares up on your genitals. The symptoms come and go, and treatment can alleviate them, but you have the disease forever. It isn't medically all that serious in most cases, but it certainly is socially serious. It means that for the rest of your life you'll risk infecting anyone you go to bed with—including your marriage partner. Try explaining that. Somehow it takes the edge off romance.

STD's are showing no signs of going away. Doctors keep discovering new ones (AIDS, chlamydia, and herpes have surfaced as big problems in just the past few years, although people have been having sex for centuries). Even the diseases we can cure, like syphilis and gonorrhea, are spreading at an epidemic rate. According to the government's Centers for Disease Control, cases of STD's have tripled in just six years. And they're growing fastest among people in their teens and twenties.

However, statistics don't make an impact. People just don't grasp the implication that they could be the next statistic. In fact, they don't even think about it. Take this girl:

A well-meaning friend (concerned about my love life) introduced me to K. K. He was not my type—#1 reason being that he is not a Christian. But he was attractive and charming, and I enjoyed the attention. We went out a couple of times while I wavered between right and wrong. He, or course, was only concerned with getting into bed. To make a long story short, we ended up sleeping together. A couple of days later, out of guilt and shame and embarrassment, I ended the connection and asked him not to call me again. I asked the Lord for forgiveness and then tried to put the incident out of my mind.

Now for the problem. Two weeks ago, I found out I have herpes. I can't undo what has happened no matter how desperately sorry I am. I've stayed awake many nights in tears, feeling cheap and dirty and unworthy of love from the Lord or anyone else.

I have only had one mild bout with herpes, and my doctor says that in 50 percent of all cases it never comes back. But, of course, that is no guarantee. So what happens when I meet the man I feel is right for me to commit myself to for life? I'll have to tell him about this incident and the consequences. Should I expect him to forgive me, even though it might be a great struggle?

The fear of duplicating her experience ought to be enough to make anybody think twice. But will they? I doubt it. After all, "Herpes only happens to other people."

ARE YOU IN A HOLE?

Often I am struck by the difference in approach between what the Bible offers and what non-Christians think it offers.

Many non-Christians see the world as a beautiful, green field with a few deep, dangerous holes to avoid. Seeing things that way, they think Christians have labeled sex outside marriage as one of those deep, dangerous holes. That's their quarrel with us, for they can see with their own eyes that people who have sex before they're married don't disappear down a hole. Rather, they often carry on with life more or less like everybody else. Their logical conclusion is that sex outside marriage must not be a deep, dangerous hole. Christians must be wrong.

But what they think Christians are saying isn't really what the Bible is talking about at all. The Bible does portray the world, as God made it, as a beautiful, green field. But we're not cavorting about that field. We've already fallen down a hole. In fact the whole human race was born in a hole because of their stubborn rebellion against God. This is clearly shown by the anger, jealousy, broken promises, selfishness, and malice that so often permeate our thinking. As to our sexuality, it's "in a hole," too, as demonstrated by broken relationships, infidelity, loneliness, lovelessness.

Jesus Christ came into the world to enable you to escape that hole. Sexually, he wants a man and woman to experience the deeply committed, spontaneously joyful, delightful relationship that Adam and Eve enjoyed. But attaining this is not easy. You can never make it on your own. There are certain activities that interfere with all attempts, and one is sex outside of marriage. When you do that, you don't fall down a hole—you *stay* down the hole. You're likely to continue with the ordinary, semicommitted, what's-in-it-for-me kind of relationships. You're less likely to rise to the kind of love that lasts forever.

God created sex for our pleasure. He made it to be the seal of a totally committed, loving, secure, lifelong, exclusive relationship—the kind of love affair that goes by the name of Christian marriage.It's undoubtedly true that nobody on this earth has lived up to the ideal God wants him to experience. But some people are moving in the right direction. Others are content to stay in their hole. ▰▰

SEX MAKES BABIES

While we're discussing horrible possibilities, let's add one almost as bad as AIDS: an unwanted pregnancy. The birth of a child is meant to be a high point of life—a glowing, rhapsodic thrill for two in-love parents. Instead, when the girl is young and unmarried, it can become a sick tragedy. If present trends continue, two out of every five teenage girls will get pregnant at least once before they turn twenty. To put it bluntly, pregnancy can, and often does, ruin their lives.

First, they lose love. Typically, the guy sticks to the girl through the abortion or, sometimes, the birth. He hangs around the clinic feeling worried, concerned, responsible. But he seldom lasts much past the end of the pregnancy. If he had wanted responsibilities, he would have gotten married. While you can love a mother with a baby, it's just not the same as going steady. Bye-bye love.

If the mother has an abortion, that usually knocks out the love affair, too. For the girl it's a traumatic affair. Nearly always she has a tremendous sense of responsibility or guilt. Often she feels she's a murderer. Suddenly the gravity of what she's doing becomes clear. *Sex is not just fun and games. Life and death are at stake.* No matter how hard he tries, the guy is on the sidelines in this drama. It's hard for him to understand. Most times he just doesn't want to handle it. He gives up and goes on his way, leaving the girl very much alone.

Besides losing the love, there is another, much more significant loss—the girl's future. For a teenage girl, a baby is a life disaster that usually knocks her out of school and into a dependent situation (either on her parents, or on welfare, or both). How else can she raise a baby? About half of all the mothers on welfare had their first baby while they were teenagers. Teenage mothers also tend to have personal problems later on. For example, their marriages are much less likely to last. Having a baby when she's a teenager is bad news for the mother. It's usually bad news for the baby, too. The child has to grow up with an unhappy mother.

There's really no pleasant solution to a pregnancy out of wedlock. Lots of girls have their babies and, rather than trying to raise them, give them up for adoption. The girls can then go back to school and continue with life. But deep pangs of regret may go with them. Bringing a baby into the world stirs up deep emotions. By nature, a mother will die for her child. When she gives a child up for adoption, she's going against nature. However much sense it makes, it hurts deeply, and keeps on hurting.

An abortion is tidier than having a baby, of course. But the memories aren't so tidy. A baby died. You were responsible. You can never forget. That hurt, too, goes deep and may never be completely healed.

But why go on? Pregnancy scares most kids half to death. When a girl's period comes two days late she feels sick with fear. Yet year after year surveys report that most kids who are sexually active don't even use birth control. I could multiply the horrors indefinitely, but does all this information convince anybody to wait? If they won't use birth control, what can make them stop sex altogether?

YOU CAN'T SCARE PEOPLE ENOUGH

Common sense says AIDS should convince a lot of people that the only place for sex is within marriage. Who wants to die? Common sense says that fear of pregnancy should do the same. But people just don't get scared of sex very easily. For hundreds of years syphilis was deadly, too, but that didn't put prostitution out of business. Sex is too basic, too strong. And people think that disasters only happen to other people. They think they will never grow old, they can never really be hurt.

It's valuable to know the real consequences of sex outside of marriage. They remind you that the picture portrayed on TV and in the movies leaves a lot out—it leaves out heartbreak, loneliness, ruined lives, infertility, disease, death. The real consequences can make you stop and think—do I know what I am doing? Sex is a life-and-death matter. Do I just go with the flow?

Yet, while fear grabs people's attention, it doesn't seem to hold it— not against the powerful impulses of sexuality. If people are going to wait, if they are to control the powerful, God-given urges of sexuality, they will need more than fear. They will need a motive that lasts, indeed that grows stronger each day.

CHAPTER FIVE

THE DREAM

Fear may get people's attention, but for motivating any sustained effort I'd choose hope.

When I was in junior high school I practiced basketball by the hour. I don't remember enjoying the practice. I was usually alone, and I usually felt frustrated because I missed the basket so often. But I kept trying. Why? Because I hoped to make the basketball team.

You practice a sport because you hope for success and recognition. You do your homework because you hope to graduate, to get a good job, to succeed in your career. Fear that the coach will yell at you or that your parents will ground you only goes so far. You'll keep on working, week after week, only if you believe it will lead you to the fulfillment of a dream. Hope is also why you comb your hair so carefully, choose your clothes so fussily, worry over your image so endlessly. You believe it makes a difference and hope it leads you to your dream partner. You hope it leads to love.

That hope often leads to sex. You're finally together, a matched pair. This is what you've dreamed of, worked for. You're half drunk with excited feelings. Finally somebody understands you, listens to you, cares for you. It feels great when you kiss, better when you caress. You can hardly contain yourself when you do this, and what everything leads to—the summit of feeling, of body-desire and soul bonding—is intercourse. Sex with somebody you love—oh, what a feeling!

I'd like to ask: Since people so often wake up from the dream in the morning with a headache and feelings of guilt, is hope enough? Suppose you dream bigger.

IMAGINE THERE'S A HEAVEN ON EARTH

Suppose you dream about the conditions. A beach? A mountain cabin? Imagine total privacy. All alone, with nobody to disturb your lovemaking. Add a kitchen stocked with food in case you're hungry. A living room to sprawl in. Why not shoot for the moon? A whole, unoccupied house—yours for making love in all day and all night. A place decorated in just the style the two of you like. With a good stereo and a VCR, if you care about music and movies to relax.

Suppose you dream, not of just one night, not of just a weekend with your parents away, but of a thousand nights. Suppose you insist on an opportunity for ecstasy every night for ten straight years. Or more. Make it thirty. There is no going home. Ever. You wake up together in the same bed you went to sleep in, night after night after night.

Dream on. Suppose there is no fear. No possibility of being caught unhappily pregnant. No possibility of disease.

And no worry about hiding what you're doing from others. In fact, you could get out of bed, shower, dress together, and go off to church, arm in arm. If you wanted privacy, you could have it. If you wanted friends around, it wouldn't be even slightly uncomfortable. And when the friends went home, you could make love again. You'd have all the time in the world.

Dream to the limit: you could practice, practice, practice, endlessly. Sex experts point out that couples need years to reach their peak. You don't achieve anything like great sex in a couple of weekends. But this is a dream: no time limits. You'd become as good as you pleased. No hurry.

But so far this dream is one-sided—the physical. The best loving depends on *who* you're with, not just *how.* So imagine you've found the best lover in the world. Dream for all you're worth.

The Perfect Lover—for You

What qualities do you want in that special person? *Who* do you want?

Not a movie star, but a real flesh and blood individual who talks to you, goes on walks with you, laughs with you, works alongside you.

Somebody you love to look at.

Somebody you love being with because you feel relaxed and have such fun.

Somebody who brings out the best in you.

Somebody who shares your sense of what's important.

Somebody you want to talk with forever.

Somebody you admire who has integrity and tenderness.

Somebody who loves you—and you trust with your life.

To find somebody who suits you like that, you'll have to do some fancy choosing. Imagine you have. After much thought you've chosen each other for this experiment in loving. There's no doubt about it. It doesn't get any better than this!

You come with total commitment to love each other, to never let go. You don't have to be jealous, or insecure, or worry about what the other one is thinking because you know. This person loves you without reservation and will never leave you. This person has decided to choose you forever and knows how to keep a pledge.

The conditions are right for this love to keep on growing forever. You have the time. You have the sexual freedom. You can open up to each other totally, without fear that if your partner knew that one dark secret he wouldn't like you. You're able to share your thoughts. You choose to share your possessions. You're working together now—to make a home, to serve God, to have children. Becoming coworkers draws you together as much as becoming lovers. You work through problems together—how to spend your money, where to spend your vacation—and grow closer. Your love grows deeper.

One more thing. If you could really live this dream, if you found the perfect person and you both were ready, wouldn't it be ideal to start it with the biggest party you've ever seen? Invite all your friends? Family? Dress up, celebrate? And to mark the solemnity of the moment, have a service to praise God and pray for the future of your happiness?

It's quite a dream. It's called marriage—the way God planned it.

The most incredible fact is this: Some people do actually get to experience this. It's not just a dream. It can be reality.

The dream called marriage is the only hope powerful enough to make people wait for sex. It alone puts all the pieces of their sexuality together. It alone is worth waiting for.

Can You Get There from Here?

God gave each one of us this dream at birth. It's part of our nature to hope for that loving, intimate, and permanent relationship with a member of the opposite sex. That's why so many songs are love songs. That's why even cynics can get sucked into a romantic movie. No matter how hardened a person becomes, he retains, somewhere, the longing for this kind of love.

However, the dream can become buried—like a spark in the ashes of a fire that's nearly out. That's what's happening to a lot of people. They still have the dream in their souls, but it's no longer something they hope for. It's just a wish. It's just a romantic, impossible dream.

Once upon a time the dream seemed real and vivid. Those were the days when girls had "hope chests" and guys went "courting." The goal of male-female relationships was undisguised: "First comes love, then comes marriage, then comes Jane with a baby carriage." You could plan on it. Not that everybody who got married lived the dream. Then, as now, there were plenty of unhappy, lonely, embittered people. But they didn't usually divorce then; they stayed married—sort of.

Nonetheless, the dream was real enough for most people to give it all they had. People saw the risks but believed it was possible to overcome them.

People still dream about marriage with great hope in their eyes, but the dream is blurred. When they look around and see so many simply living together without benefit of commitment, when they see so many marriages crumbling, it's harder to focus on the dream. It's still there, but far off, indistinct. They can't, it seems, plan for it; they hope to luck into it.

People become almost fatalistic about love. They pledge to stay married "as long as we both shall love"—as though the end of love just happens like catching a cold. People divorce because, they say, they've grown apart, they've discovered they are incompatible. If that happens, it's just too bad. They can't give a relationship something they don't feel, so they move on.

The dream however, does not depend on luck for fulfillment. You can make it happen if you're persistent and prayerful and if, instead of focusing all your attention on how love feels, you pay attention to the kind of character that lasting love demands.

You don't have to be seven feet tall to achieve the dream of marriage as God intended it. You don't need a high IQ. You don't even have to be physically attractive. It is usually very ordinary people who achieve the dream. A lot of extraordinary people don't.

However, the dream does expect certain things of you. It is worthwhile, but it isn't free.

Q: Until about a week ago, I used to laugh at the kind of advice you give. I was one of your so-called "semi-Christians." You know the type—you believe that you're a true Christian to the core, but actually you're just a Christian when you feel like it. You know sex feels great, and if it feels great then it must be all right. Those righteous know-it-alls who say to wait are just jealous because they don't get any. And hasn't anybody heard about the sexual revolution? So you get a lot of friends who are girls, and you take them out and have sex all the time. That's what they're there for and you know it and they know it, too. And let's not forget the parties you get drunk at. They're the best. After all, these are your high school years, and that's what you're supposed to do when you're a teenager.

Yeah. My life summed up in one paragraph.

But there was a flip side, too. The part that made me a semi-Christian. I believed in God and I'd accepted Jesus Christ as my Savior. I did my best to obey his commandments—at least the ones I felt like obeying at the time.

But all that's changed now. I took this girl to the drive-in. We were going to a camping-out party afterwards. The way she was acting made it rather obvious what she had in mind for that night. It was the typical routine until I got her to the party. All of a sudden I was scared. Afraid. And most of all, I felt guilty. I just had to get away. I made up some excuse to go home, and then I ran all the way.

When I got home, I just needed to sit down and think. *Campus Life* was sitting next to me, so I picked it up and started to read. Then everything you said made sense. I was cheating myself. I had been having sex because I was lonely and it seemed the easiest way to get attention. The odd thing was that the more I had sex, the lonelier I had been getting! And here was God, giving me a second chance. He loved me and was offering to be my special friend. I had been a fool. But I would be a bigger fool if I turned him down. So I didn't.

I've lost some "friends" because of what I've given up. But I've made new ones—true friends who love me for what I am, not for what I do. Thank you for helping me and others see the way. And thank you, God, for being a friend in need.

A: I appreciate your writing, not just because of your thanks but because of the message fresh from the other side. I'm sure plenty of people who struggle to follow the Christian way wonder sometimes whether it's worth it. They occasionally *are* tempted to be jealous; the people who party and mess around seem so brash and confident. They seem to have so much fun.

There's more to that story, though. You've given us just a part of it. The way you've chosen leads not only to true friendships but to true sexual fulfillment later on. The way you've left? I believe you've already experienced the best it has to offer. It leads nowhere. ■■■

CHAPTER SIX

WHAT THE DREAM REQUIRES

Think back to the dream we conjured up and you'll see that some of the requirements are built in. For instance, a one-night stand, however wonderful, doesn't qualify for the dream. If one night is good, wouldn't two nights be twice as good? Wouldn't a thousand nights be a thousand times as good? The best, obviously, would be a lifetime together. That's the dream: the very best loving human beings are capable of.

Requirement #1: The dream goes on forever. If you're really seeking the dream, you'll *commit* yourself to a lifetime, and not just hope you luck into it. People in the dream don't ever say good-bye.

Sometimes, because you're not perfect, the dream may run into long dry spells. That's reality for human beings. Commitment pulls you through so you can reap the happiness on the other side. The fact that you may go through dry spells and stay depressed for days at a time shouldn't be allowed to wreck the dream.

If you can't make this kind of commitment, you're not ready to live the dream.

Requirement #2: The dream calls for self-sacrificing love. When people first fall in love, they don't need to be told to care for each other's good. They can't do enough for each other. They're always thinking about each other. That makes them both happy. But sadly, concern doesn't last. Each person drifts back into being selfishly preoccupied. So there needs to be commitment to keep that concern for the other going strong and to keep the happiness flowing. Commitment means to put your partner's needs ahead of your own. You have to give, even when you don't feel like it. This is true love—it isn't just a feeling. It's much stronger than any feeling; it's strong enough to carry you across deep rivers.

Requirement #3: The dream must have no competition. You can live the dream with one person only. Try it with two, and—poof!—the dream disappears.

You can give all of yourself to only one person. Give even a small piece of yourself to a second person, and automatically you're not giving all of yourself to the first. That's arithmetic. This exclusivity applies over time, too. You can't just drop one dream partner and start with another as though it made no difference. The old partner stays with you. That person's memory lingers, and competes. This is peculiarly true when you have been sexually involved. In sex you give yourself body and soul to another person. *Give,* not loan. Part of you remains with your partner, and part of your partner clings to you, even if you never meet again. You're like ghosts haunting each other's lives.

Requirement #4: The dream must begin with a moment in time when you make total commitment. You can't ease into the dream. One moment you're holding back, thinking about it. The next, you're in it forever.

Naturally, before you commit yourself to the dream you'll have a relationship, perhaps a very loving relationship. But that's not the dream. So long as the relationship is on a trial basis, you can't give all of yourself. You have to hold something back. You have to maintain your independence—after all, the relationship may be over tomorrow. When you give yourself to the dream, however, nothing can be held back. And between the state of noncommitment and the state of total commitment there is a single point in time. One moment you're still able to draw back. The next, you're committed.

It's like standing at the top of a tough ski run. Naturally, if the run is really difficult, you're scared. You've known all day you were going to try it. But even as you lean forward on your skis, you're still able to go back. You can back off. You can take some other run. Then, with a deep breath, you push off.

That's how every marriage is. In one sense a relationship grows very gradually, almost imperceptibly, as you get closer to each other. But total commitment does not grow gradually. It's sudden. One moment it's not there. The next it is.

People often think they're more committed than they really are. I know I did before I got married. The wedding was planned. The invitations were out. We were both in our late twenties, so we felt quite old and mature. Yet two weeks before the day, I found myself sitting on a log in a mountain forest, listening to the woman I loved as she sobbed and told me she didn't know whether she was cut out for marriage.

We did get married and have lived as happy a marriage as I am able to imagine. But I will never forget the sudden flash of fear that stopped my heart as I realized one thing that day: You aren't married until you're married. Total commitment happens at a specific moment—and not one moment sooner.

IS MARRIAGE REALLY A DREAM?

These requirements sound tough. When you're dreaming of endless love and endless pleasure, you don't want to think of commitments and duties. Yet sometimes that's what marriage sounds like—a long list of rules and expectations.

Married people don't always act like people living a dream existence. If anything, they seem rather bored and tired. Is marriage really a dream?

Not necessarily, no.

But potentially, yes.

If I had to claim that every married person is living a dream existence, experiencing the total sexual fulfillment God created them for, I'd deserve to be taken away in a straitjacket. Lots of married people are miserable. Lots of them haven't experienced any ecstasy in years.

Marriage isn't the dream. It's the foundation of the dream. It gives you a chance—your best chance—to live up to your potential for boundless love and ecstatic sex.

While it's true that not all live up to their potential, it's also true that many do.

Marriage sets the conditions for maximum love and maximum sex, but it doesn't guarantee them. That's up to you. Living the dream depends on the quality of your character. Can you really love another person, even when it hurts? What about the person you choose? Can he or she love you back the same way?

It takes a lifetime to answer these questions. It takes a lifetime to live the dream.

You won't get the chance, though, if you don't meet these basic requirements: commitment for a lifetime, commitment to sacrificial love, commitment to love one person alone—and a single moment when you take the plunge.

CHAPTER SEVEN

WHAT ABOUT RIGHT NOW?

I want to be frank about this so please understand. About nine months ago we made love for the first time. Ever since then we've made love many times, growing in our openness and willingness to experiment. It's brought us very close. Now that I know what sex is like, I feel like it's really no big deal. I used to think it was terrible to have sex [before] you were married, but now it doesn't seem terrible at all.

Marriage is *someday.* Your God-given wiring says, "*Right now.*"

Is it possible to enjoy loving, joyous sex with your partner today, and still someday make that big commitment to marriage? Why should one interfere with the other? To discuss this very practically, let's take a typical case.

RICK AND JUANITA

Rick and Juanita fell in love in chemistry class. Juanita noticed him first. She had always liked the looks of tall, skinny guys, but that soon became a forgotten preference. Rick was a mid-sized, muscular jock whose neck had disappeared into his shoulders. She talked with him after class once and realized, about midnight, that she hadn't stopped thinking of him since. She'd been shocked by his sense of humor; she hadn't known a jock could laugh at himself.

In the library the next day Juanita sat down next to Rick and asked him how to solve a problem. She made a point of talking with him whenever she got a chance. Three weeks later the phone call came.

Within a month they were going out each weekend, sometimes twice. He invited her to his church. Soon they were deeply in love. Some of it was physical—a lot of hormones were flying. The overwhelming feeling was that they matched each other—they cared about the same things. They could talk freely to each other. Rick was so kind and thoughtful. He would call up just to say he loved her. He brought her a shell from the beach. They were soon far past holding hands and kissing. It didn't seem wrong, it seemed warm, close, intimate. They couldn't get close enough. They talked vaguely, dreamily, about marriage someday.

The more immediate question was when they would go all the way. Rick had the greatest hesitation. He had been raised in church and accepted the teaching that sex was meant for marriage. His faith meant a lot to him. Juanita, whose mother sometimes invited men home, was less worried. Though she had never yet had sex, she had long assumed she would with someone, sometime. Her mother was going to be out of town on a business trip over the weekend before Rick's birthday. Juanita thought it would make a lovely present for Rick—and for her—to have their first time together then, and she proposed it to him. He felt his breathing tighten just thinking about it.

The Pros and Cons

What should Rick and Juanita consider? What are the issues?

Hardly a word would be needed in favor of making love. The electricity speaks for itself. If it were cheap sex, casual sex, it might be harder to justify. But these two loved each other, and they're not really kids any more. Since they're both virgins, disease isn't a problem. They would plan on using a form of birth control. Why not do what they're wired to do? Why not go all the way with their love?

It probably would feel wonderful. It probably would give a powerful sense of closeness. (That's not guaranteed, of course. Sex can be painful, and confusing, and guilt-producing, as many would testify.) It would certainly satisfy, at least temporarily, their sexual drives.

Those are strong arguments for going ahead. The arguments for waiting would have to be stronger. Stronger than biology. Stronger than the natural urges of love.

The only force that strong is the dream.

They've already begun to think of it—vaguely, dreamily. This bliss they're in may not have to end. It may not necessarily be merely a teenage love affair. Their love is just awakening in them. They are both beginning to hope bigger things than going steady. They are beginning to hope the dream. And they don't want disappointment to rudely jolt them out of it. They don't want to discover it was all a joke. They want to live the dream forever.

What does that mean for Rick and Juanita? It means they should keep sex out of the picture until they are ready to marry. Why? Two reasons: to protect the person they are growing to love, and to magnify the love they are beginning to experience.

PROTECTION

When you love someone, you want to protect that person from all harm—including any possible harm *you* might do. Immature lovers don't care about protection. They drive faster, brag about sex, even enjoy hurting their partner just a little. Real lovers slow down, defend their partner's reputation, try never to say anything hurtful.

Waiting until you're married to have sex is the best protection you can offer someone you love.

Protection from Pregnancy

Pregnancy can be a major disaster, particularly for a girl. It can ruin her life. It can ruin their love.

But Rick and Juanita would use birth control. Doesn't that eliminate this problem?

No, it does not. The only safe birth control is abstinence. All other birth control methods fail, regularly. (Take a poll of married couples sometime and ask how many of their kids were planned.) Condoms, for instance, which are the most popular birth control method for teenagers (and the method most effective in controlling the spread of diseases like AIDS), have a 10 percent annual failure rate. That means that if you use them, the chances are one in ten that you'll have a baby on your hands within the coming year. That's a whole lot better than the odds for those without protection. But 10 percent per year is not precisely safe, any more than one bullet in a gun with nine blanks is risk-free. When you're talking about a disaster of this magnitude, "fairly safe" is not good enough. How safe should you keep someone you love? As safe as humanly possible.

If you're in love, you want to protect each other—and protect your growing love—from the disaster of an unwanted pregnancy. But very strangely, few kids use even failure-prone birth control methods. Surveys indicate that they know where to get birth control supplies, but they just don't like to think about such stuff in advance. If they're not concerned about such basic protection, how much do they really love each other? No doubt they *feel* great love, but love is more than feelings.

Of course, Rick may say to Juanita in all sincerity, "I love you. If anything happens, we'll just get married." But even if he lived up to that, it wouldn't be good protection either. In the old days it was felt that a boy owed it to a pregnant girl to marry her. Maybe he did owe it to her, but very often it worked out to be no favor. To live the dream, you need to marry when you're ready for it. "Ready" is not the same as "capable of conceiving a child." Most shotgun marriages break apart. That's not the dream—that's the nightmare.

There is no absolute protection from these disasters except the protection of waiting for the wedding day. Rick owes that protection to Juanita. Juanita owes it to Rick. They both owe it to the love that is growing between them.

Protection from the Domination of Sex

One of the problems with sex is it feels so good. This is not a problem if you are living the dream. It is a joy—in marriage. Sexual attraction keeps drawing you back together, even when you're upset. But if you are not married, the good feelings of sex can take over your relationship. Ultimately they can ruin it.

Here's a typical description:

> *More and more, it seems as though there's only one purpose to our relationship. Nowadays we don't find a lot of time for talking or many subjects to talk about either. I sometimes wonder if we even love each other any more, or if we've become just a habit. We have talked about this problem and said that we would only have sex once every other week, but that just seems to make us more edgy together, and we always end up doing the same thing. I don't know what to do. We're stuck in a pattern we can't escape.*

That's the kind of letter I've received many times. Nobody yet built a relatonship on sex. Sex should be an expression of married love. Sex doesn't create love. Yet sex is so powerful, it can grow to dominate your relationship so that you spend all your time and energy on sex instead of doing wholesome things together that will make your love grow. When you try to change the pattern, you discover that you can't. You thought *you* were in control, but now you realize that *sex* controls *you*.

People like Rick and Juanita often approach sex as an experiment. They think they can have a weekend together, see how it feels, and then (fully informed) decide what to do. It doesn't work that way. You can't try sex to see whether it's good for you. Once you start it, you'll almost certainly continue it until you break up.

Oftentimes the bond of sex will last even after the relationship has been destroyed. Both people know their love is over, yet sex keeps drawing them together. That's how strong it is. Consider what one person wrote to me:

> I have a big problem. About four years ago I met a really nice guy who had just moved to my neighborhood. He was the first guy I really loved, and the first guy who really loved me back. We started going together about six months after he moved here. We had a very serious relationship—we were sexually active.
>
> We broke up one year ago, but we're still sexually active. We still care about each other a lot, but not enough to be doing this. Besides, it's wrong.
>
> He goes away to college this fall. I don't know if that's good or bad because I couldn't imagine never seeing him again. I still care about him a lot. He's my best friend. I'm very jealous of him and other girls he sees or dates. I feel I have a right to be.
>
> I want to be happy, but it's been so long since I have been! We've tried to stop having sex, but so far it hasn't worked. I've prayed, but nothing seems to help. I don't have anyone to talk to. I have learned a lesson, though: sex can be a very bad habit if you start it when you aren't with the person you will be spending the rest of your life with.

Rick and Juanita get together for long periods only once or twice a week. They need to talk together during that time, to laugh together, to work together, to build the basis for love. A relationship that doesn't get nourished grows stale. Sex alone won't feed it. Couples who might have stayed together if their relationship were growing instead find themselves drifting apart.

Protection against the Agony of Splitting

When people in love go to bed, there's self-surrender involved. They're naked and totally exposed before each other. The act of love is not just a uniting of bodies, but it is also a uniting of minds and spirits. There is a spiritual exchange even in the most casual one night stand. You can't really have sex casually. It's not a casual thing. Your spirit is involved.

That's why rape or sexual abuse are such hideous crimes—they rape and abuse the spirit.

People who have given themselves to each other should never have to take the gift back. People who have experienced sexual unity should never have to split. Any loss of love is painful, but losing love after you've given yourself body and soul hurts horribly.

It hurts to find that someone you trusted and loved so much is now hardly more than a stranger to you. It also hurts, and keeps on hurting, to know that someone you don't love anymore, who means little to you now, knows every inch of you.

There's no way Rick and Juanita can know, at this stage, that they'll never break up. Feelings change. If their relationship comes apart after going to bed together, it will hurt horribly, deep inside. Lovers should protect each other from such a loss of love and the psychological hurts that will follow.

That's what one girl discovered the easy way. She wrote to me:

> *Three of my best friends are sexually active. I sat and cried with each of them a few weeks after their first time and prayed with each of them that they weren't pregnant. Don't get me wrong. They weren't "bad" girls, and they didn't take sex lightly. They were all good Christians who thought they were giving their most precious gift to the men they would marry. But sex is no promise of marriage, and all of these relationships are now history.*
>
> *I don't judge my friends for what they did. I would have done the same thing a year ago had I been dating someone I loved. I was able to learn from my friends' mistakes. Now I know without a doubt or regret that I will experience the joys and wonders of sex only when I am married.*

Making love makes you so vulnerable that you need the strongest protection that human beings can offer—the protection of a wedding. When you're ready to make a commitment to each other for life, you set a day to go public. The wedding makes a promise before God, before family, before friends, before the community. It marks a total change of life. You move in together. You begin sharing money, plans, possessions.

A wedding doesn't guarantee you'll never break up. But it's the closest thing to a guarantee that society has been able to invent and is even more so when it's between two people with a sincere and deep trust in

God. Such a ceremony is certainly far more trustworthy than private, whispered promises. A private promise won't do when you buy a car or join the army. You have to sign. You have to publicly pledge. Why should less be expected of those making the most important commitment of their lives?

What do you promise in your wedding vows? Basically this: "You're the one I'm choosing to spend my life with. You're the one I will love, protect, and honor, not just today, but tomorrow and forever." If you can honestly make those promises in public, before God, you're ready for the vulnerability of making love. If you can't honestly make those promises yet—at least, not publicly—that's a very good argument that you're not yet ready to expose yourself and your partner to the possibility of a soul-shattering loss of love.

Protection from the Descending Spiral

Virginity is, to many in our times, an outdated word. To be a virgin is to be considered naive, left behind, out of touch. Virgins are in the "out-crowd." They don't know what's going on.

Down through the centuries, however, people have seen something precious and beautiful about virginity. It's time we recognized it again. A virgin *is* different from a nonvirgin. They *don't* know what's going on. They're vulnerable. They're open. They're untouched.

Virginity doesn't mean "left out." It means "still waiting, still looking, still expecting." That's a good way to be until the day you seal your future with the person God gives you for a lifetime of sexual fulfillment. If you want to bond with someone so strongly that nothing can break the bond, it's best to bond as a virgin. That way no past experience must be erased. No other influences need be undone. You experience all the embarrassment, excitement, curiosity, uncertainty and discovery of the first time with the only person in all the world you want most to share such a wonderful and intimate experience.

When you make love for the first time you break a psychological and emotional barrier; sex will never seem so strangely mysterious again. It soon becomes comfortable, normal. If you're living the dream, that's fine. You don't need any barriers.

But if you're like Rick and Juanita, it's a problem. There's no guarantee your relationship will last. The descending spiral begins when that first, intimate relationship breaks up. Both of you, suffering from the loss of love, are vulnerable. In your sadness, you look for comfort. You find it, often, in the arms of another person. People call it "on the rebound." And if you've had sex before, sex becomes amazingly easy. After all, the barriers are down. Sex has become "no big deal," to use the words of the girl whose quotation begins this chapter. Surveys indicate people who are sexually involved with one partner seldom give up sex when the relationship ends.

Of course, love on the rebound is not usually the stablest kind. So a few months later you find yourself with a sexual history—two past partners. That changes your outlook still more. More barriers are down. You're on your way down the descending spiral.

A lot of people end up with a sexual history that takes hours to tell. Once the barriers were down they just kept on going with one partner after another. Maybe they even got married and then divorced, but the marriage was merely part of the downward spiral. Each time sex got easier; each time it meant less. It's not impossible that they'll someday turn and ascend the spiral, capturing the dream. Some do. It's just less likely.

If you love someone, you want to protect that person from this spiral. You want to protect yourself. And until you're ready to provide the protection of wedding vows, you should provide protection by not breaking down any barriers. Let them stay high. Or if virginity was previously broken, let the downward spiral stop with you.

Q: I am twenty years old and I am a virgin. I have been dating my boyfriend for about two years. A couple of months into the relationship he told me he wasn't a virgin. I understood and accepted it then. Now it is finally hitting me. We are both Christians, and we plan on getting married in a few years. I've forgiven him for what he did yet I am having a hard time struggling with this. I love him very much, yet sometimes I think that our honeymoon won't be special because of what he did. I have prayed about it and I have tried to forget about it, but I'm still confused. My question is: Should this really bother me as much as it does? If not, how can I stop it from bothering me?

A: Yes, it should bother you. The current idea that sex is a pleasant get-acquainted exercise for potential lovers would suggest that nothing very big happened between your boyfriend and his nameless bedmate of the past. But that's not true. Sex is the deepest, most intimate exchange two people can make. It affects them deeply, and they carry the memories—good or bad—for the rest of their lives. So naturally you are bothered to know that someone you love has been to bed with someone else.

Sure, if people live in a promiscuous society long enough it may stop bothering them. But *should* it stop bothering them? I don't think so. When it stops bothering you, it's probably because sex doesn't mean as much to you.

That's not the same, however, as saying that your boyfriend's past has to ruin your future together. The past can't be ignored or undone, but it can be *forgiven*. Forgiveness is a mystery, really—a grace which God alone can give us. I don't know how to tell you to forgive your boyfriend, or how to get that forgiveness to penetrate to the bottom of this barrier. But I do believe it's what needs to happen for your relationship to go forward.

Really, it is a question of love. If you love your boyfriend deeply enough, that love will enable you to cover over his past mistake—not by ignoring the pain he's brought you but by weaving it into a bigger fabric of your relationship so that ultimately you are tied together more strongly than ever. If that happens, your honeymoon will, indeed, be very special. Special in its own way—flooded with the depth of your forgiveness and love for him. ■■■

Protection from Ghosts

Sex is more than just a nice thing to do for an evening. Sex is spiritual. It affects you to the core of your being. It takes two people and bonds them so that, as the Bible says, they become "one flesh." Even if you try to keep it impersonal, as in a one-night stand, that experience—that partner—will remain with you for the rest of your life. The partner won't be a living, loving presence, however. The partner will hang on as a ghost.

By "ghost," I mean memories so strong you can almost touch them—memories that interfere with life. Take this guy, who feels haunted:

My first girlfriend was quite aggressive. I was a little on the shy side, but she initiated all of our sexual activity. I hardly knew her, and I knew I didn't love her, but she was nice and attractive. We dated three months, and then she decided she wanted to go out with other guys.

Today, three years later, I am in love with a sweet and caring Christian girl. The problem is, I did things (we masturbated each other) with my first girlfriend that I feel very dirty and guilty about. I'm sorry and have asked the Lord to forgive me, but I still feel dirty inside. I worry, too, about whether to tell my new girlfriend about it.

One of the commonest questions people ask me is, "Will I have to tell my future spouse about my past?" I don't favor compulsive candor. For instance, I didn't advise the guy I've quoted to tell his new girlfriend all about his past. When marriage comes into the picture, however, there should be complete openness. True oneness keeps no secrets.

Regardless of whether people tell or don't tell, however, the ghosts will be with them. Some people take ghosts on their honeymoon. They have to either explain those ghosts to their new spouse or else continue to worry about them.

Marriages should not be haunted by ghosts. It's too easy to be jealous of that phantom, to wonder what really went on between your spouse and former lover. If your partner keeps old letters and photographs from another relationship, you're bound to feel some twinges of jealousy. You can burn letters, but nothing can destroy memories.

If you love someone, you want to protect your living the dream together without ghosts. That means don't become a ghost yourself.

WHAT IF RICK AND JUANITA GET MARRIED SOMEDAY?

Suppose that Rick and Juanita become sexually involved, keep it from dominating their relationship, and go on to form a wonderful marriage. Would that make their sexual involvement before marriage right? If it all works out, is there any harm in their sexual involvement?

It's hard to answer that question, because it's so hypothetical. The main issue is this: When Rick and Juanita were considering what to do about sex, they didn't know how their relationship would turn out. So their decision must be based on what they know, not on what they don't know. If all turns out well in the end, that doesn't make their decision to have sex before marriage right.

Relationships *can* work out in the end for couples that make wrong choices. Rick and Juanita may make the wrong choice and yet still go on to live the dream together. They could even split up after being sexually involved, and by the grace of God go on to live the dream with other partners. Nobody's life is ever really hopeless. Nobody is disqualified from living the dream because they made a mistake.

But the dream of love is too important to take needless risks. If Rick and Juanita really care about each other, they'll want to protect each other from the risk of pregnancy, from the domination of sex, from the agony of splitting apart, from the descending spiral, and from ghosts.

However, their decision about sex involves more than protection. It also involves positive qualities they should be building into their relationship—qualities that matter for a lifetime.

CHAPTER EIGHT

MAGNIFYING LOVE

Protection is mainly negative. It takes seriously the possibility that a relationship may not last forever. But it's hard for Rick and Juanita to imagine such a disaster. They love each other so strongly that their love blots out fears.

Are there *positive* reasons for them to stay out of bed right now?

A BETTER RELATIONSHIP

What could be better than sex? But people who aren't married get more out of their relationship if they stay out of bed.

They have more time to get to know each other. The basis of the relationship is clear when you're not sexually involved: *This is a trial. We're getting to know each other. We're learning how to enjoy another person, how to care for another person. But we don't belong to each other, body and soul.* Realizing this helps couples avoid the emotional and psychological traps waiting to ensnare those who go too far.

It's true that many couples say sex initially brings them closer together. The closeness is superficial, however. It's only body-closeness—complete with its powerful emotions. Because it's not matched by commitment, anxiety lurks under the surface. *Where is this leading? I say I love her—but do I really mean that?* As we saw in the last chapter, the relationship can fall apart even while the sex continues.

Those who aren't sexually involved experience a much greater sense of freedom in their relationship. They aren't committed; therefore they can enjoy each other without strings attached. They can get to know each other without feeling caught. They know that their love, if it grows, isn't based just on physical attraction. As one girl wrote, "I've recently become engaged to a real nice guy. I'm glad to say that he asked me to marry him without knowing how I am in bed. In other words, he asked me because he loves me."

THE HONEYMOON

There is a qualitative difference between a wedding day for virgins and a wedding day for the sexually experienced. Virgins may be twice as nervous as nonvirgins on their wedding day, but that's good. You ought to be nervous on the biggest day of your life. For virgins, everything is about to change. They will enter, that night, into mysteries they have wondered about all their lives. And they will do it right. That's worth celebrating.

For a couple who've been sleeping together, the wedding is something like a graduation ceremony: For the person who finishes school a semester early, graduation is just a ceremony. The exercise may be enjoyable, but it lacks punch. For the person whose classes just ended, graduation is a *celebration*.

Similarly, the honeymoon for virgins is unique, unrepeatable, incredible. For the sexually experienced, a honeymoon is merely a nice vacation.

You get only one "first time" in life. There is great joy in experiencing it with the person to whom you've just publicly committed your life. But that's only possible if you wait.

TRUST

Living the dream means a total, lifelong commitment. You have chosen one person. Nobody else will ever be a competitor. That security and trust is essential for a truly intimate relationship.

It's possible to live the dream even if you don't both enter it as virgins. Some people do. They experiment with several partners, then eventually settle on one, live together for a time, and then marry. It's possible their commitment could grow to become total, and they could learn to trust each other. But that's the hard way to get there. And for every one who makes it, a lot more don't. When you've grown used to low-commitment sex, it's hard to switch to total-commitment sex.

Surveys indicate there is wide-spread cheating in marriage today. People who learn to take sex lightly before marriage tend to continue to do so after marriage. Consequently, many marriages are plagued by suspicion and jealously. *Is she going out on me?*

If before marriage sex merely meant, "I'm strongly attracted to you," it is not easy to change body language after marriage to mean "I give myself wholly to you."

Those who wait show each other that they take sex seriously. They demonstrate the kind of discipline and self-control every relationship needs. That builds trust. It builds respect. Take Rick and Juanita's case, for instance. What would happen if Rick decided to say no to Juanita's weekend plans for their sexual encounter? She might feel disappointed initially. But eventually her respect for Rick would grow. She would develop deeper trust in his ability to make a right choice even when it's hard, and would admire his self-discipline. She would almost certainly feel proud that he loved her enough to want to protect her from risk— even if she were willing to take the risk herself.

If they go on to other relationships, Rick and Juanita won't have a sexual history to admit to. Their next partners won't worry about competing with past partners. There won't be any ghosts to be jealous about. Trust, which every lasting relationship must have, will be able to grow freely.

If Rick and Juanita do marry, they'll be able to give themselves fully, freely, for the first time to the one great love of their lives. That builds trust.

If you want to experience total-commitment sex, the surest way is to experience no other kind. It's hard to wait for, certainly. But most good things are.

Q: I'm a fourteen-year-old freshman, and my boyfriend is a sixteen-year-old sophomore. A few days ago I went to a school dance and we left the dance and got really physical. We didn't have sex, but all the other things we did made up for not going all the way. He asked me to make love, but I said no because I was scared to.

I love my boyfriend very much. We've set a date a few weeks from now to go out with some friends, and from what they've told me we're going to make out (in other words, go all the way). I'm really scared to, but I'm afraid if I don't then I'll lose a little bit of my boyfriend. He always says he loves me, and when he holds me I feel so good like I'll stay with him forever and everything will be great. My real questions are: How do I know when is the right time? And how do I know if he's the right guy? And how is a really sure way to find out if he really loves me as much as he says he does and as much as I love him?

A: I'm glad you asked. I'm glad to answer because I have a pretty clearly formed philosophy about your three questions. Let me take them in order.

First, how do you know when is the right time? You know it is the right time when you and the person you love have both stood in front of all your friends, family, and God and promised to be married for the rest of your life. Then you go off to live together—forever. Then sex is as right as right gets. Weddings are not foolproof, but they're the best indicator yet invented that you're ready for the huge involvement, spiritually and physically, that sex inevitably brings.

Second, how do you know if he's the right guy? There are many factors to consider in evaluating a guy, but ultimately it comes to this: you know he is the right guy if he will stand in front of that crowd (mentioned a paragraph ago) and make those solemn vows, and if you want to be there doing the same thing with him. Some ringers get past this test, but it is amazing how many it eliminates.

Third, how do you know if he loves you as much as he says he does? You can judge this most accurately by asking him to put his life on the line by standing in front of all those people (twice mentioned) and making those promises. People do lie on their wedding day, but not nearly so many as hand out big lines when they're making out like mad after a dance.

I realize that living by this standard may mean disappointing your boyfriend. But, as hard as this may be to believe, if you lose him over this the loss wasn't that terrible. It is indeed a wonderful feeling to be held close by someone and to feel in love. But you can get that feeling on a temporary basis with many people. You won't keep the feeling with anyone, on a long term basis, unless you use your sexuality very wisely. Your body is too precious, and the nakedness of sex too absolute, to be given on any basis less solid than marriage. ▬

PERFECT TIMING

There's a right way and a wrong way to get something done. A lot of it
has to do with timing. If you go off the high dive with your timing slightly off, you'll still end up in the water. But you won't get there with maximum smoothness and beauty.

There's an inherent rightness in waiting for the wedding day. It's the
rightness of timing. You go all the way with your body on that special
day when you go all the way with your mind and with your heart. You
say "I do" and the full freedom of the dream begins. It's not the only way
to get into the dream, but it's the surest, the smoothest, and the most
beautiful.

The media have flooded us with a distorted picture of what's beautiful: beautiful bodies; clever speech; impetuous, erotic romance. "To-
night's the night," the advertisements say. They don't worry about
tomorrow.

But what is truly beautiful is the whole dream—a lifelong love between two people bonded to each other until death. A love that grows
and deepens day by day and year by year. A love that brings fulfillment,
where sexual needs are met without fear or guilt. A love that's secure
and lasts a lifetime.

That beauty begins with the growth of a couple's emotional love—a
love that wants only the best for each other. And though this may grow
into a desire for physical intimacy, they choose to wait, to remain inex-
perienced until they are sure—sure they have chosen the best person to
be their partner for life.

When you love someone, only the best will do. Waiting for the wedding day is the best.

CHAPTER NINE

WHY DOES GOD SAY TO WAIT?

There is another reason to wait for marriage in addition to the ones already mentioned. For those who believe in God, it is the most important reason: God teaches us to wait.

Why? Why should it matter to God? For one reason only—he cares about us.

It's odd how little weight God's Word receives. Most people in America say they believe in God. Most people say they consider the Bible to be God's Word. But if you stood up in many classrooms and proposed following God's Word as it relates to sex, people would react as though you were a prude and wanted to outlaw happiness. You'd have to explain at great length why God's Word is really good for people, and God's plan for sex the best.

The need to justify God is a little crazy. Were Wilbur and Orville Wright against air travel? Of course not! Neither does God consider sex to be anything but a joy and a blessing. After all, it was his idea. He could have made us to reproduce like plants. Imagine: you take a piece of fingernail, cover it with potting soil, water carefully—and in nine months out comes a baby.

God didn't want to do it that way. He preferred that all human lives spring from the exultant, loving embrace of sexual intercourse.

The all-knowing God who invented sex should know how it can best be celebrated. He loves us. He sacrificed his own Son to redeem us. He wants what's best for us and wouldn't arbitrarily spoil our fun.

Who Needs Advice?

There's another slightly goofy aspect to this. People get indignant at someone bringing religion into the picture. They suggest it's because Christians are so sexually repressed they want to make everybody else just as miserable as they supposedly are: "Christians just aren't happy as long as someone, somewhere, is having a good time."

But where exactly is this party that Christians want to spoil? Some individuals are having fun, but a lot of people are having a miserable time. You can't cut the statistics to read any other way. Millions of divorces, adulteries, and abortions add up to something other than fun.

Unfortunately, people are so used to thinking of sex as it comes to us in *Playboy* that they can't see it any other way. The *Playboy* philosophy in the movies, magazines, and certain TV shows portrays sex as fun, sensual recreation. It's one big party. They're right, sex *is* fun. But they leave out the results of sex that are quite common: broken hearts and relationships, tragedy, loneliness, jealousy, frustration. Not to mention unwanted pregnancies, abortions, and sexually-transmitted diseases. Most people's lives bear little resemblance to the carefree life-styles promoted in *Playboy*.

God isn't trying to break up our party; he's trying to help us. When God gives direction, he does it either to protect us from harm or to provide for our needs—or, as in this case, both.

WHAT DOES GOD SAY?

The word *puritanical*—which means severe or strict—does describe some Christians. They seem to think it's a sin to enjoy themselves. Some, even though married, want to keep sex very tame. They might have been happier if God *had* made them like plants.

God, however, is not puritanical. The Bible, our best guide to God's mind, is very frank about sex. There is not a prudish verse in it. A whole book (the Song of Solomon) celebrates the sensuality of erotic love. It's certainly nothing like pornography. You wouldn't read it to get turned on. However, you might read it to see how wonderful God intended sex to be. The Song isn't tame. Neither are the lovers who sing the song to each other.

Overall, sex is not a big subject in the Bible. Other topics—particularly our relationship to God—take precedence. When the Bible does discuss sex, however, it reflects exactly the attitude you'd expect from an inventor writing about his invention. The inventor, better than anyone else, appreciates what his invention means. He's happy to speak of it. He understands how it works and knows exactly what it's good for. He doesn't overload you with instructions, but cuts to the heart of the subject. He tells you how to put his invention to practical use.

And this Inventor is very firm about his ideas. He doesn't spend a lot of energy explaining why things are the way they are. He just insists: this is the way it works!

The Bible's view of sex can be put very simply: Sex is wonderful within marriage. Outside marriage, it's an offense to the Inventor.

It says in Hebrews 13:4: "Marriage should be honored by all, and the marriage bed kept pure."

Pure means "unmixed with any other substance." You could paraphrase the message this way: "Set your hopes and dreams on marriage. Allow only one person into your marriage bed—your husband or your wife. Don't adulterate that relationship with anyone else."

The Bible recognizes that sexual desire is a strong physical urge. It presents marriage as the normal answer to that: "Since there is so much immorality, each man should have his own wife, and each woman her own husband. . . . Do not deprive each other except by mutual consent and for a time, so that you may devote yourselves to prayer. Then come together again so that Satan will not tempt you because of your lack of self-control" (1 Corinthians 7:2, 5).

But marriage is much more than a license for sex. Marriage is designed to help us experience what we long for: a bond of totally committed love.

When Adam was first made, he lived alone with the animals. Up until that point, God had pronounced every single thing he had made good. But when he saw Adam alone, God had a negative response: "It is not good for the man to be alone" (Genesis 2:18).

So he made a woman, Eve. When Adam saw her, nobody had to tell him she was made for him. He practically shouted it: "This is now bone of my bones and flesh of my flesh!" (Genesis 2:23). With her true intimacy was possible. Through her the "not good" of being alone was changed. With her Adam could become "one flesh." Genesis closes the description with this phrase: "The man and his wife were both naked, and they felt no shame" (2:25).

That's the way sex is meant to be and the way God designed us. Marriage isn't just a convenient way of producing children, but it's a special union where we can find all the love we need. It's a solution to loneliness. It's a relationship where our deepest longings can be satisfied.

The love we're called to have in marriage should be modeled after the deepest, most intimate love in the universe: "Husbands, love your wives, just as Christ loved the church and gave himself up for her. . . . Husbands ought to love their wives as their own bodies" (Ephesians 5:25, 28). That love is the kind of selfless love Christ had when he gave himself as a sacrifice to redeem mankind.

Yet that love is unmistakably sexual. Marriage as God designed it is a love feast for the whole person, body, soul, and spirit. The Book of Proverbs, which was written as advice for a young man, puts it this way: "Rejoice in the wife of your youth. A loving doe, a graceful deer—may her breasts satisfy you always, may you ever be captivated by her love" (Proverbs 5:18-19). God doesn't want to spoil our party. From the beginning, knowing our needs, he set out to provide a party.

Falling Short of the Dream

The dream, as set out in the Bible, is this: total nakedness, total unity, total love, total sexual satisfaction. God intended us to be happy.

But the Bible minces no words about behavior that tends to destroy the dream. Plenty of marriage problems parade across the pages of Scripture showing how people mess up their own happiness. Jesus, particularly, made his views on that plain. Though he never married, he spoke with absolute authority (like an inventor) against abuses like fornication, adultery, and divorce: "Out of the heart come evil thoughts, murder, adultery, sexual immorality, theft, false testimony, slander. These are what make a man 'unclean'" (Matthew 15:19-20).

"What God has joined together, let man not separate. . . . Anyone who divorces his wife, except for marital unfaithfulness, and marries another woman commits adultery" (Matthew 19:6, 9).

Jesus didn't go into a lot of detail. You could sum up his teaching quite simply: Sex is for marriage. Marriage is for life. Anything that breaks that dream apart—whether it's adultery, or casual sex, or divorce—is falling short of what God intended.

Jesus warned us not merely to stay away from actions that destroy the dream. He included our thoughts in his uncompromising indictment of abuses: "You have heard that it was said, 'Do not commit adultery.' But I tell you that anyone who looks at a woman lustfully has already committed adultery with her in his heart. If your right eye causes you to sin, gouge it out and throw it away. It is better for you to lose one part of your body than for your whole body to be thrown into hell" (Matthew 5:27-29).

Paul, who wrote many of the New Testament letters, dealt with problems new Christians had. He showed the same absolute attitude that Jesus did: "Put to death, therefore, whatever belongs to your earthly nature: sexual immorality, impurity, lust, evil desires and greed, which is idolatry. Because of these, the wrath of God is coming" (Colossians 3:5-6).

"The body is not meant for sexual immorality, but for the Lord. . . . Do you not know that your bodies are members of Christ himself? Shall I then take the members of Christ and unite them with a prostitute? Never!

"Flee from sexual immorality. All other sins a man commits are outside his body, but he who sins sexually sins against his own body. Do you not know that your body is a temple of the Holy Spirit, who is in you, whom you have received from God? You are not your own; you were bought at a price. Therefore honor God with your body" (1 Corinthians 6:13, 15, 18-20).

THE SAME MESSAGE TODAY?

The Bible puts it strongly, without waffling: Give all you have to marriage. Make it your dream. Pour into it your love and faithfulness. And run away fast from anything that goes against that dream.

The only question is: Does this advice still apply? After all, the world has changed.

The first changes you might mention are birth control and medical cures. At least, people used to bring this up in the days when the Playboy philosophy was flying high. You sometimes hear it still, in a form something like this: "In the days when sex automatically led to babies, sex had to be kept limited to marriage so that the kids would have a home. Nowadays a couple can use birth control, so their sex life is their own business; it doesn't concern anybody else. Monogamy was necessary before when syphilis was deadly. But now that it's curable, there's no reason for two healthy kids not to do some sexual experimentation."

The fact is that, even with all the advances in birth control, we are seeing far more babies born out of wedlock than ever before. Birth control could greatly reduce that problem, but it usually isn't used. Even when it is, the failure rate is high enough to be scary. As to the cure for syphilis—AIDS is a much more frightening replacement.

It's interesting to note that there's not a single line in the Bible mentioning babies as the reason to abstain from sexual immorality. Babies are always a blessing in God's eyes. Babies aren't the cause of God's strong concern about sex outside marriage. The Bible's concern about sex outside marriage is simply that *it's outside marriage.* It doesn't belong there. "Marriage should be honored by all, and the marriage bed kept pure." Sex outside marriage doesn't honor marriage, and it certainly doesn't keep it pure.

BUT ALL THESE YEARS OF WAITING!

One reason some give for having sex before marriage is that people in Bible times married young. They didn't have the long gap we do between puberty and marriage, so they didn't face long, difficult years of waiting. They didn't date. They didn't fall in love in high school and then have to wait for marriage until they finished college. So it was much easier for people to be faithful to God's plan for marriage.

The only trouble with this explanation is the fact that people in Jesus's day found God's directions hard. Impossibly hard. When Jesus explained that for Christians there can be no divorce except on the grounds of sexual unfaithfulness, his disciples (hand-picked by Jesus, remember) replied bluntly: "If this is the situation . . . it is better not to marry" (Matthew 19:10).

Even though they lived in different times, the disciples showed by their response that people still had marital problems. Since they married young, their parents had a great role in picking their partners. They married at thirteen or fourteen, perhaps, and were expected (by Jesus) to live the dream with that same person forever. Apparently, some of the men found that the bride who was a joy to them at fourteen somehow didn't satisfy them at twenty-four.

It's hard to live the dream in any culture, in any age. Whether you're unmarried and waiting, or whether you're already married and trying to make your love work, you'll feel frustrated at times. When people get frustrated, the grass looks greener on the other side of the fence. Unmarried people think, *If I just had sex, I'd be happy.* Married people think, *If I just had another partner, I'd be happy.* Surely this was also true of those in Bible times who married young. They often fooled around. They often divorced. Otherwise, why would Jesus bother to warn against such things?

For them, as for us, there was only one way to achieve the dream: make no compromises. Keep yourself pure and be faithful to God's plan for marriage.

Why? Because God said so. Not only does he know more than you, but he loves you more than you can ever comprehend. He wants your marriage bed pure because he cares for you. He wants to protect you from the worst. He wants to provide you with the very best.

Sure, it's hard. It demands sacrifice and self-control. What good thing doesn't?

ISN'T THE BIBLE ABOUT LOVE?

Another "times-have-changed" argument goes this way:

"When the Bible talks about 'sexual immorality' (which the older translations call 'fornication') it's talking about prostitution or other kinds of sex that are totally unloving. In those days there was plenty of cheap sex available. It was nothing like today where two people may love each other but have to put off marriage because of school or other causes. The Bible calls people to love each other above all else. That's the highest good. So when two young people in our society sincerely love each other, their love makes sex more legitimate than a piece of paper ever would. It certainly has nothing to do with what the Bible calls 'sexual immorality.' There's nothing immoral about love!"

So the argument goes. To some extent, I would agree with it. Love really is what sex is all about. But what I do have trouble with is this: Two people who become "one flesh," "naked and unashamed," are meant to be bonded together forever. If they are so in love that they know for certain they'll never break apart—that their love is so committed nothing but death can separate them—then they're ready to go all the way with their love. But love—committed love—makes it right first.

How can they show that they have that kind of love? The best test is for them to step into a church, to a ceremony before God, before their families, and before their friends, where they will solemnly pledge that kind of faithfulness. And the marriage license makes their union official before the eyes of the community. So it's a good thing.

The trouble with *love* is that it's a vague word. By love, some people mean a feeling. They think that a tremendous rush of emotion would justify any deed. The Bible certainly doesn't teach that. But if by love you mean committing your life to another person, the Bible certainly does teach that. That's what the dream is all about. The wedding ceremony is our society's way of separating those with only strong emotions from those with also strong commitment.

Q: You stress that premarital sex is wrong and give biblical verses such as Matthew 15:19, 1 Corinthians 6:9-10 or Colossians 3:5-6 supporting *your* opinion. However, these biblical verses never state that premarital sex is wrong, they just say stay away from sexual sin. How are we supposed to know what is sexual sin and what is not? With all the hate and war in this world, making love does not seem sinful.

A: Good question. Since the Bible was put together almost two thousand years ago and was written in Hebrew, Aramaic, and Greek, the advice it gives isn't always easy to translate directly into modern American English. That's unusually obvious in this question of premarital sex. Times have changed, and we have to ask how advice written then applies today.

The immediate problem, which you've caught, is translation. You (and I) would prefer it if the Bible said flat out, "No premarital sex allowed." But there isn't any New Testament Greek word for "premarital sex." The word the Bible uses, which gets translated "sexual immorality" or "sexual sin" (or "fornication" in the older translations) is *porneia*. Not all scholars agree on how *porneia* should be translated, but the most common belief is that it's a broad word that could be applied to specific situations. "Casual sex" might be a modern way to put it, or "sexual immorality."

At first glance, it looks as though the word *porneia* is so general it doesn't help at all. As you put it, how are we supposed to know what is sexual sin and what is not? But if you look carefully at the whole New Testament's teaching about sex, things become a lot clearer. The New Testament presents only one proper place for sexual intercourse: within marriage.

In those days most people old enough to be interested in sex were already married. If they weren't and didn't want to be, prostitution or adultery were the obvious alternatives for sexual intercourse. But both of these are labeled very clearly as wrong.

Adultery is wrong (Exodus 20:14). Casual sex with prostitutes is wrong (1 Corinthians 6:15-17). Single people who lack sexual self-control are urged to marry, not to practice "safe sex" (1 Corinthians 7:2, 9). There weren't any other alternatives. In all of the New Testament you don't find a single hint of an exception or loophole. In fact, Jesus says that even *looking* with lust is as wrong as adultery (Matthew 5:27-30).

If your question is, Why doesn't the Bible say premarital sex is wrong? the answer is it does. It sets marriage as the ideal—and any sexual activity outside marriage as wrong. For Christians in the early church, the broad word *porneia* was evidently clear enough. They knew what it meant, just as our grandparents didn't require an interpretation of "sexual immorality." They understood that included all sex outside marriage.

The real question doesn't concern what the Bible says about premarital sex, but whether the Bible is relevant today. Would it be wrong for two people who really love each other but aren't ready for the commitment of marriage to make love? Maybe the people who wrote the Bible never thought of that. Personally I doubt they did, any more than they imagined teenagers driving around in cars on Saturday nights. However, I can't see any reason to imagine they would have felt more positive about sex outside marriage in our situation than they thought of it in theirs.

What makes premarital sex in our situation different? One answer people give is birth control. However, 1.5 million abortions, and even more children born out of wedlock in the U.S. last year, would suggest that sex and pregnancy go together as much as ever.

Even if they didn't go together it wouldn't change the Bible's position. There's not one single word in the Bible about babies as "unwanted." Pregnancy can be a problem for us, but it evidently wasn't in biblical societies. The Bible's concern is about what happens *spiritually* between two people who have sex. (First Corinthians 6:12-20 and 1 Thessalonians 4:3-8 take this up in the most detail.) Those spiritual realities aren't changed by contraception.

Other people say that what makes premarital sex acceptable in our time is love. They point out that in New Testament days sex outside marriage meant either cheating on a marriage (adultery) or some kind of sex for money (prostitution). Today two people may sleep together because they feel powerfully swept up in love. Isn't that different? Doesn't love make it right?

It is different, but I can't see why the difference would have made any difference to the biblical writers. While Paul urges married people to develop a loving relationship (Ephesians 5:25-33), it's very obvious that the love he's talking about is committed for life. He's not talking about powerful, temporary emotions, but commitment to serve and care for each other, regardless of what comes. He's talking about the kind of love God shows us, which doesn't run out tomorrow—or ever. That's true love. Within it, sex becomes beautiful and holy.

Why is it so important to have this commitment before sex enters the picture? Because sex, by its very nature, makes a commitment. That's why Jesus was so opposed to divorce: "They are no longer two, but one.

Therefore what God has joined together, let man not separate" (Matthew 19:6). Sex bonds two people together, whether they intend it to or not (1 Corinthians 6:16). When this bond is broken or when the bond is unsuitable in the first place (as it is with a prostitute), deep injury is done.

I must answer one more point from your letter: "With all the hate and war in the world, making love does not seem sinful." I guess that takes us back to your own question: How are we supposed to know when something is immoral and when it isn't?

One fact the Bible shouts loud and clear is that, by ourselves, we're not very good judges. We tend to justify whatever we do and condemn what others do. Take a look at all that "hate and war" you mention, and see whether you can find anybody who really believes he's at fault. The Iranians blame the Iraquis, the Iraquis blame the Iranians, the Arabs blame the Israelis, the Israelis blame the Arabs, the Catholics blame the Protestants, the Protestants blame the Catholics—and nobody ever takes the blame himself. That's why God's Word is so valuable. It tells us, independently of our own emotions and self-justification, how to judge ourselves.

Making love outside of marriage may seem rather innocent, compared to some things that go on, but that doesn't make it right. Shoplifting at the mall may seem rather innocent compared to armed robbery, but that's a weak justification for shoplifting. If you play the comparison game you can make everything short of the Holocaust seem innocent. Our thinking about sexuality can become so warped that even sin begins to look normal.

I could make a good argument that premarital sex is as destructive as any force in our society today. All those abortions, all those unwanted children (who contribute tremendously to crime, drug addiction, and the horrible poverty cycle of people—particularly women and children—being stuck in the ghetto), the widespread sexual unfaithfulness and divorce and broken homes, and the plague of AIDS and other sexually transmitted diseases—don't those have anything to do with innocent premarital sex? It doesn't seem farfetched at all to see that the Bible's warnings against sexual immorality remain relevant today.

Q: I am a nineteen-year-old virgin. It has not been easy to stay this way, but I am a very disciplined person and I have managed to control my actions. I felt pretty good about myself until I read Matthew 5:27, where Jesus tells us that anyone who lusts after a woman with his eye has already committed adultery in his heart. I have found it totally impossible to keep from thinking about sex, especially when I am around females. It seems to me that this passage also tells us that masturbation is wrong because when a person masturbates, he or she is thinking lustfully and is usually fantasizing about someone in particular.

This means that from the time I reach puberty (twelve to fourteen) until the time I get married (probably about twenty-five, at the earliest) I am not only supposed to keep from having or thinking about sex, but I can't even masturbate, not even once. Why would God create all this sexual energy in me and never allow me to release it? I find this to be totally unnatural, illogical, impossible, and ungodly. I feel extremely guilty. I am severely depressed and I don't know if I even believe in God at all. I have even started avoiding girls to keep from thinking about sex. Please help!

A: I believe you've misunderstood what Jesus said, though it's a misinterpretation lots of people make. If you look at the context of this verse, you will see that he took up a whole list of topics—murder, adultery, revenge, generosity, prayer, fasting—and went through it attacking the attitudes of religious people who thought they had it all together. Jesus said their goodness wasn't good enough. People who were proud of themselves because, for example, they had never committed adultery, needed to see that their thoughts and desires were meant to be as pure as their actions.

"Be perfect," Jesus went on to say, "as your heavenly Father is perfect" (Matthew 5:48). If we had been able to live up to that, Jesus wouldn't have had to die on the cross for our sins. None of us can live up to all God expects. As far as lust is concerned, every human being has had sexual desires that are wrong. Some of us may not need forgiveness for our *behavior,* but all of us need forgiveness for our *desires.* I have wrong desires, you have wrong desires, your pastor has wrong desires. They're not wrong just because Jesus said they were wrong, they're wrong because they're evil and destructive. Rather than feeling good about ourselves, we're to come closer to God in recognition of our constant need for forgiveness and healing. That's the first point I want to make. Don't get angry at God because he expects the world of you. Come closer to him. Learn that you can't live without him.

I'm not saying, however, that we aren't to try to obey Jesus's commands. I believe you've misunderstood the command. *Lust,* in English, usually suggests mental pictures about sex. In Greek, though, the word *epithymia* doesn't have that connotation. It just means "powerful desire." It's not even a negative word. It can be a beautiful desire, as it was when Jesus told his disciples at the Last Supper, "I have eagerly desired [lusted] to eat this Passover with you" (Luke 22:15).

So you have to look at the context to understand what *lust* really means. That's not crystal clear in Matthew, but it seems to mean "committing adultery in your heart." Your heart, in the Bible, isn't composed of thoughts that flit through your mind. Your heart is your core identity; it's the direction you choose to point your life. I think Jesus is referring to times when you "would [commit adultery] if [you] could."

Suppose you go out with a girl. You get sexually excited, to the point you're ready and willing to go all the way. But something stops you. Perhaps it's fear. Perhaps it's *her* willpower. Perhaps you just got interrupted. How do you think about yourself afterward? Some would think, *I'm a flawless human being. I have never failed.* If they heard about other people who were sexually involved, they'd feel superior. To them, Jesus is saying, "Oh no. You're no better than they are. You wanted to do it. Your heart is just as rotten as theirs. You need God's healing and forgiveness just as much as they do."

This kind of lust could happen for someone you don't know—a beautiful girl you watch every day in class, thinking about what you'd like to do with her. Are you better than the person who actually does it? No. You'd like to do it, so you need forgiveness and help, too. Your actions aren't wrong, but your desires are.

That's what Jesus is getting at, I believe. I don't think he's trying to get you to stop being a sexual creature. I don't think he's suggesting that when you look at a beautiful girl you should avoid sexual attraction. I don't think he's talking about masturbation. I think he's talking about your heart—that is, the fundamental desires you choose to center your life on.

When sexual thoughts come into your mind, it's quite possible to thank God for beautiful girls and for sexuality and just feel good about being alive as a male in a world full of beauty. You can imagine how wonderful it will be to someday be married. That's good and healthy, I believe. There's nothing evil about those desires.

What's not good is to take those thoughts and build on them, obsess yourself with how much joy you'd get from going to bed with one of those girls. Whether you act on your desires or not, you've made sex into something less than God intended. Jesus doesn't want you to turn off your sexuality (even if you could). He wants you to channel it in the proper direction. He wants you to turn your thoughts toward him.

Why didn't God make it easy to please him? Why not give us sexual desires on our wedding day and not before? Why not take away our attraction to certain people of the opposite sex? Why not, for that matter, take away our tendency for greed, so that we wouldn't think somebody else's

Porsche was particularly attractive? I don't know. You can play the "Why-didn't-God-do-it-differently?" game for a long time, and not come up with any answers. I do know *I* wouldn't like to be without sexual desires. I like being a human being, hard as it is. I'm thankful God trusted me with the challenge. I'm equally thankful that God picks me up when I fail to live in my life the way I should and ask him for forgiveness. ■■■

CHAPTER TEN

HOW TO SAY NO

I dated a lot my first semester in college, but all the young men seemed to be the same. They all told me they loved me, but really what they meant was "I want you."

Kids who get sexually involved often say peer pressure played a major part in their decision. How can that be? In most cases, sex is something two people decide to do under very private circumstances.

Peer pressure comes in two forms. First, as we discussed in an earlier chapter, it affects your thinking about what's acceptable. Most people prefer the safety of the crowd. Few like to be different. So if you figure all your friends are sexually involved, you'll feel pressured to be like them. At the very least, when you're tempted, you'll think of your friends and rationalize, "Why not?"

The other form of pressure is more direct. It comes from a member of the opposite sex. Your boyfriend (or girlfriend) wants to go all the way. Even if he says he "respects your beliefs," you feel pressured to change your beliefs, even though you sincerely want to wait for marriage. The pressure of the crowd or the pressure of someone you're going out with may get to you. You need to learn how to say no.

GOING AGAINST THE CROWD

You aren't likely to singlehandedly change the sexual beliefs of your school. Being in the minority isn't easy. Especially when you feel the strong influence of TV, movies, and music going against you.

But you may not be in such a minority as you think you are. Those who consider sex a normal part of adolescence tend to speak up about it. Sometimes they brag. (Some bragging, of course, is wishful thinking.) Occasionally they're downright insulting to those who take another point of view—calling them prudes, or teases, or accusing them of hypocrisy or naiveté. That can be intimidating.

On the other hand, those who think sex should wait for marriage tend to consider the subject private. They don't make a lot of noise about their beliefs. So they usually appear less numerous than they are. Surveys indicate a large group believe sex should wait for marriage. However, some surveys indicate the majority of kids believe that sex is all right as long as two people love each other. This means a significant number of kids feel it's right to become sexually involved before marriage.

Going against that crowd takes courage. Here are three ways to strengthen your beliefs:

1. Write out your philosophy of sex. It may help to first read some Christian books on the subject. Then try to put it into your own words.

When somebody's discussing the subject, ask yourself: *What would I say here? How would I answer these questions?* Even if you never open your mouth in a public discussion, you'll learn to think clearly what you believe and why.

2. Find some friends who share your philosophy. You may find them in an organized group such as Campus Life, Young Life, a school club, or a church youth group. Or you may simply find them one by one. Break the intimidated silence. Share your philosophy of sex with them, and ask them to tell you what they believe. If possible, agree to support each other in prayer. It's unfortunate that most people only talk about their philosophy of sex with someone they're dating. A group of peers who share your philosophy can provide *positive* peer pressure.

3. Put sex on your list of prayer concerns. Make it a daily prayer— whether you're under pressure or not—to be helped and guided on your way to living the dream. Too often prayers deal only with immediate requests. Pray long term. Pray about your whole life and its direction.

Some people have found it helpful to pray each day for the person God will lead them to marry. Though they don't know who that person is or what he or she is like, they pray that their future partner will grow deeper and stronger in character, closer to God, and be protected from temptation.

Pray also for yourself: that you'll be growing, too, so that when and if you marry, you'll be prepared to live the dream.

SAYING NO TO A SPECIAL PERSON

It would be better if you never dated or got romantically involved with someone who doesn't share your basic values. But to be perfectly realistic, it's a possibility. Sometimes you will like that person so much you'll go against your better judgment. Sometimes, too, you just won't know his or her true values until you're involved. People don't usually write their sexual philosophy on their T-shirts.

As two people grow in love, they feel increasing pressure to lower their moral standards. Sometime you may even get involved with a person who seems to suddenly change his values. In the excitement of the moment, with loving emotions flying high, he may toss his "wait-for-marriage" ideas out the window. Then you'll experience real peer pressure—pressure from someone you care about—someone you may even love.

People have a hard time saying no to a special person for two reasons. First, they don't know what to say. Many have only the vaguest notion that they want to stay a virgin until they get married. When someone asks why, they can't answer. It doesn't take much to convince them to change their ideas since they had no definite beliefs to begin with. Their well-wired body will certainly take charge from there.

If, however, you have a clear idea of what you believe, you can defend it and stick to it. That's why being able to articulate your philosophy of sex is helpful not only in saying no to the crowd, but in saying no to someone you're starting to love.

The second reason people fail to say no is that their self-image is too weak. They're afraid that saying no will cause them to lose the person they're beginning to love. So they give in.

I got a panicky letter from a girl who was desperate for help. She wrote:

> *I'm nineteen and am going with a guy who's the same age. I'm in another country right now and the distance has brought us closer. He says that he loves me, and I love him, too. In one of his letters he wrote, "I believe that you can write 'I love you.' But what I'd like to see is proof of it when you get back."*

The guy pulled out the oldest line in the book: "Prove your love by going to bed with me." And she was scared to death! Why? Because she didn't want to lose his love. She was terrified of his demand, but she couldn't imagine how she'd survive if he didn't like her response.

She needs self-respect—enough so she'll demand respect from others. She needs enough confidence to gladly tell such a guy to get lost. What makes him so wonderful that she should have to "prove her love" to him? Let him prove *his* love by showing respect.

There's no store where you can buy self-respect. You can't order it from a catalog. No magic formula will give it to you. You give it to yourself. You do that because you know you deserve it, because God made you and loves you and intends to give you more goodness than you can handle.

Q: I've recently become engaged to a real nice guy. I'm glad to say that he asked me to marry him without knowing how I am in bed. In other words, he asked me because he loves me. I love him a lot, too. We have started getting closer sexually than I ever thought we'd get. We started petting— not a lot, just once in a while. Lately I've wanted to go further, and he has, too. Neither one of us feels pressured. I guess you could say we're just interested. Are these feelings of interest wrong? Sometimes I want to make love with him because I just feel so comfortable with him. I know he wants to, also, but I'm glad that when I say stop or no he doesn't lay a guilt trip on me. Sometimes I don't want to say stop. What should I do when these feelings come up?

A: You certainly shouldn't feel guilty. There's nothing wrong with these "feelings of interest." Rather, there is a great deal of right in them. Such feelings are part of getting ready for marriage. Half the fun of a celebration is the anticipation leading up to it. That's why we make such a fuss about the Christmas *season*. If Christmas Day just popped up every year without anyone thinking about it in advance, it wouldn't be half as much fun. Do you remember the agony of waiting when you were a little kid, looking at those packages under the tree and wondering what you would get? Do you remember how time slowed down to a crawl? That is not too different from what engaged couples feel. You only get married once. It ought to be so exciting it makes you slightly nauseous!

Yet that excitement also makes it hard to handle. It is hard to wait for sex; doubly hard when you are in love and already committed to marriage. So how should you handle your desires? The answer is simple but not easy. When you get those feelings, get up and take a walk. Do something different. Go shopping. Go bowling. Call up some friends and plan an activity with them. Don't try to *fight* the feelings—*dodge* them. And make sure you keep yourself out of similarly tempting situations in the future.

Also, you can transform that feeling into other ways of love when you're alone. Use your creativity: Write a poem, compose a song, paint a picture, pick some wild flowers.

It's not easy to wait. But it's worth it. A honeymoon is God's gift to you when you're unwrapping packages that are completely new. It's not as exciting to unwrap gifts you opened and used a month before. ■■■

OTHER PHILOSOPHIES OF SEX

Sometimes it's hard to defend your own philosophy. Others will nearly always be able to ask questions you can't entirely answer.

Certainly, the Christian philosophy I've put forward isn't sheer bliss. It calls for self-control when you'd rather do what feels good at the moment. Inevitably, some people won't want to buy that.

But what about the alternatives? People pushing other sexual philosophies will not be able to answer all the questions, either. It helps to realize that all philosophies offer pain as well as pleasure. When you look at life as a whole, you find that the alternatives offer a great deal of pain—and not as much pleasure as would appear.

The Playboy philosophy applies the rule of pleasure to each and every situation. Does it feel good? Does it do no obvious harm? Then go ahead and do it. The standard line of a Playboy philosopher is, "Why should I deprive myself?"

The weakness of the Playboy philosophy is that those who follow it think short-term. They don't invest in the future through discipline, self-control, and hard work. They live for the moment. And those who live their lives by the pleasure principle run into a lot of pain, in the long run. (They miss out on the greatest pleasure, too—a love that goes deeper than a centerfold.)

Playboys don't build strong marriages. They don't even build strong relationships. Playboys end up lonely. That may seem very far away right now. Years may go by—even decades—before the short-term gain of the successful playboy turns into long-term pain. But it happens. Casual sex-for-pleasure leads to casual (and callous) relationships. And that leads to loneliness.

For our society as a whole, the Playboy philosophy produces plenty of pain. Consider the millions of abortions and unwanted babies. What about the poverty of most unwed mothers? What about the women who end up worn out and rejected, their good looks gone at forty? And what about the children who will never know a father? What starts out as pleasure produces scars that last a lifetime.

The Love philosophy applies the rule of love the way the Playboy philosophy applies the rule of pleasure. By the Love philosophy (probably the most common philosophy today), sex is not justified just because it feels good; it's only OK for those "who really love each other." For how can love be wrong?

The weakness of the Love philosophy is that it's so vague. What is love? One survey found that over half of American thirteen-year-olds believe they have experienced it. How would you prove them wrong? Another question asked fifteen-year-olds who were sexually active whether they planned on marrying their partners. About half the girls said they did. But 82 percent of the guys said they did not. Obviously, the guys' and girls' perceptions of their relationships were different.

Yet, undoubtedly, those girls (and probably the guys, too) felt powerful emotions. Isn't that love? In theory it sounds natural to affirm sex between those "who really love each other." In reality, without a yardstick to measure love, those "who really love each other" turn out to be those who get emotionally involved—which includes just about everybody. The Love philosophy ends up being practiced very much the way the Playboy philosophy is. "If it feels good (loving, that is), do it." The results—short-term relationships, loneliness, the downward spiral of sexual promiscuity—are anything but loving.

The Experimentation philosophy makes a distinction between two phases of life. In the first phase a person experiments with his sexuality. In high school, college, and early single years he isn't ready to settle down, so he tries sexual experiences on for size. As long as he uses birth control and tries to be "responsible," anything goes. Later, when he gets old enough to settle down, he begins to follow a different set of rules. Rather than experimenting, he seeks to marry and stick to one partner.

One weakness of the Experimentation philosophy is that it's a putdown for kids. It suggests they don't know what life is all about, they're just playing sex games. They're not capable of real discipline or of developing the character they'll need throughout life. Their relationships aren't significant, really. They're just in the sandbox, building sand castles. "They can't hurt anything; let them play," this philosophy says.

Yet life doesn't work that way. The way people behave at eighteen will shape the way they live at twenty-eight. Life is a continuous line. Today is connected to tomorrow. A person who has never made a commitment in his life seldom develops into a totally different person later in life.

Sexual "experimentation" isn't really possible. No experience leaves such a lasting mark as sexual intercourse. Those who spend their teenage years experimenting have made the worst possible preparation for a life of real love and commitment.

PRESSURE LINES

Much of the time, philosophy has nothing to do with the pressure people put on you. They're not asking honest questions, but attempting to manipulate you into doing something you wouldn't do otherwise. If the questions keep coming, if the pressure continues, you'll have to confront it for what it is: a line.

What do you say when someone puts on the pressure? Sometimes you need to break down your philosophy into bite-sized chunks:

The line: "If you really love me, you'll show it by giving me all your love."

The answer: "If you really love me, you'll show it by never again asking me to go against what I believe."

The line: "It hurts to love you so much and yet hold back from expressing that. I feel so frustrated."

The answer: "Love is worth some sacrifices."

The line: "It will make our love grow."

The answer: "I'm concerned with what it grows into."

The line: "It will bring us closer."

The answer: "Like it does people in Hollywood?"

The line: "Every other girl [guy] does it."

The answer: "Then go out with her [him]."

The line: "Don't you think that our love makes it right?"

The answer: "No, I think our love makes it right to wait until we're married."

The line: "What could be wrong with something so loving?"

The answer: "The loving feelings are fine. It's the feelings that come when the love is all over that concern me."

The line: "We're going to get married. What difference does it make whether we make love before or after the ceremony?"
The answer: "Probably about the same difference it makes whether you practice medicine before or after you graduate from medical school."

The line: "Nobody's a virgin anymore."
The answer: "So you think I'm nobody?"

The line: "You must be frigid."
The answer: "The way you're treating me gives me the chills."

The line: "Don't worry, we'll stop before we go too far."
The answer: "Don't worry, we already have."

The line: "We'll just do it this one time."
The answer: "When I do it one time with someone, I plan to do it a thousand times more."

The line: "I'll make sure you don't get pregnant."
The answer: "No, please, I'll make sure I don't get pregnant. I use a method that's 100 percent sure—abstinence."

The line: "We have such a beautiful thing going. Why should we deprive ourselves?"
The answer: "Isn't that what Eve asked Adam?"

The line: "No, really, what's the point in waiting?"
The answer: "Have you ever tasted the difference between an apple that's ripe and one that's still green?"

The line: "You don't know what you're missing."
The answer: "That's right. In fact, have you ever noticed? *Nobody* knows what they're missing. You don't know what you're missing, either."

The line: "If you're going to be so uptight, you may lose me."
The answer: "Is that a threat? Losing someone who threatens me would be more gain than loss."

The *best* answer for someone putting on pressure: *"Good-bye!"*

Q: I went with a guy for four years, and we really loved each other. All through the four years we slept together, although I was a Christian and knew it was wrong. Since then we have broken up and gotten back together. It hurt so bad when we broke up that I knew the only way to get rid of the hurt was to turn to God. It helped, and I became a much stronger Christian than before—except for not having enough faith to say no to sex. We have gotten back together and sex has been an uphill battle for me ever since. My boyfriend is a Christian, too, but he sees no wrong in us making love as long as we love each other.

Another thing is that I'm not sure that I love him, but I feel we need to stay together because it says in the Bible that when two people make love they become one in God's eyes. Does that mean if I am to do God's will, I should stay with him because God now sees us as one?

I know the logical answer to my question about sex is to have more faith, but how can I get that through my boyfriend's head? And how can we pull together and fight this urge? We have talked about it a million times and it never helps.

A: I'm afraid I don't think "more faith" is the logical answer to your question. The logical answer—at least, the practical answer—is for you to break up. The pull of sex, particularly when it has long been a normal part of your relationship, would be extremely difficult to resist even if you both were agreed. And as long as your boyfriend sees nothing to worry about, you won't succeed. I have never seen it work.

Thus your choice is a hard one: continue as you are or split apart. Either one is painful. The way you describe your current situation, however, makes me doubt that your relationship has a good future. And the reason you give for staying together isn't a good one.

Where in the Bible did you read that people who have sex become one in God's eyes? What the Bible says is that sex makes people "one flesh." That is not the same as being married. If it were, then Paul's advice to people involved with prostitutes would have to be, "Go and find that prostitute you slept with and move in with her." His actual advice is just the opposite: "Flee." (See 1 Corinthians 6:15-20.)

For married people, becoming "one flesh" is a wonderful thing—sexual intimacy strengthens and supports their commitment. In a subtle but powerful way their lovemaking molds them together. But between two people who aren't even sure they love each other and who have made no lasting commitment the intimacy is terribly misplaced. It is like two wild animals of different species that are chained together: They don't belong together, they aren't committed to being together, but they are held together by the emotional and spiritual power of what they are doing. The relationship rarely leads to a good marriage, and the wearing of the chain can make deep wounds into both of you, leaving scars that may last a lifetime. ■■■

CHAPTER ELEVEN

FINDING FORGIVENESS

In January a speaker at our church talked about being proud of being a virgin. This bothered me very much, so much that I began to cry. I talked to my boyfriend, and he told me not to worry about it because to him I am still a virgin. Yet I was raped of my virginity.

I've met a man, a wonderful man, who has forgiven me for my past, but yet I can't forgive myself.

Can you become a virgin again? It sounds ridiculous. Why not ask, while you're at it, to relive last summer? Yet many do ask this question. "I've asked God for forgiveness. I've learned my lesson the hard way. Now please tell me how to answer people who want to know. Can I say that I am a virgin?"

The correct answer to the question, "Are you a virgin?" is: "None of your business." Or you can ask, "Why do you want to know?" Usually the person can't even pretend to have a good reason for prying into your personal life. The question is just curiosity or cattiness. A lot of time it's a put-down. If you're a virgin, you're a stupid prude. If you're not, you're "no better than anybody else." Either way, you lose. So why enter the contest? Keep your private matters private.

Even if you tell no one, though, what do you tell yourself? If you want to start over, is it possible? Can you be a virgin again?

A NEW BEGINNING

A man once posed a similar question to Jesus. "How can a man be born when he is old? Surely he cannot enter a second time into his mother's womb to be born!" (John 3:4). Jesus answered by talking about a second, spiritual birth. "Flesh gives birth to flesh, but the Spirit gives birth to spirit" (John 3:6). You can lose your physical virginity just once. If you did it, you did it. A second chance is not a first chance.

But spiritually it is quite possible to start all over again. That doesn't mean you forget all the physical and emotional consequences of your past. Spiritual rebirth doesn't erase the past. It transforms it. A second chance, spiritually, means there are no limitations to what you can become. The God who made the universe out of nothing can take the raw material of your past and make something beautiful from it.

The Apostle Paul was referring to this kind of transformation when he wrote to a group of Christians in Greece. They had plenty to regret, but because they were Christians that past had been transformed. "Do not be deceived," Paul wrote. "Neither the sexually immoral nor idolaters nor adulterers nor male prostitutes nor homosexual offenders nor thieves nor the greedy nor drunkards nor slanderers nor swindlers will inherit the kingdom of God. *And that is what some of you were.* But you were washed, you were sanctified, you were justified in the name of the Lord Jesus Christ and by the Spirit of our God" (1 Corinthians 6:9-11, italics added).

You were washed. Gently, warmly, your wounds have been bathed and cleansed. Your wounds are now healing, not growing worse from an infection.

You were sanctified. That is, you are now free from sin. You are holy in God's sight and have been set apart for his special use. He has chosen you.

You were justified. You are made right in the eyes of God. You are good enough for him, therefore you're good enough for anybody.

That, surely, is a new beginning.

The Transformation

How do you begin that kind of transformation? You can't manage it on your own. You need God's power. And where do you find that? You ask for it. It's as simple and as powerful as that. God is very near to you. Spiritual transformation begins as simply and as mysteriously as opening your mouth and speaking to him. You ask God to forgive you and change you, and God goes to work. He forgives you. He makes you right with him. He washes your wounds and begins to heal them. And you become a new person with God's help.

If you've experienced that, can you call yourself a virgin? That is a question of terminology. How do you best describe your new beginning?

To say "I'm a virgin" is confusing. A better word, which specifically refers to the state of your spirit, is *virginal*, meaning like a virgin—full of expectation and hope and innocence. You can't change the facts of your past, but you can change the way they affect you.

That may not clear up your reputation. But it does clear up your future. You are as good as new. In your life, the dream has come alive again.

FEELING GUILTY

Christians believe that forgiveness comes quicker than the speed of light. The painfully hard work was done long ago, when Jesus died on the cross for our sins. Because that's complete, forgiveness and a new beginning are given instantaneously to all who ask sincerely.

But if you've been sexually involved, the memories live on, and often with them a sense of guilt. Oddly enough, people who felt guilt while they were sexually involved sometimes feel overwhelming guilt after it's over.

So what is guilt? And what are guilt feelings?

Guilt is an objective fact. Either you've fallen short of what God expected you to be, or you haven't. The facts aren't changed by how you feel about them. Guilt feelings are your internal, emotional response. They aren't always reliable. Some people never feel guilty. Some feel guilty when they have done nothing truly wrong. Some feel guilty long after God's forgiveness has canceled the guilt.

What we call a guilty conscience is often a mixture of feelings: of regret, of loss, of sadness, of self-reproach. Those are natural feelings for someone who has been heavily involved in a relationship.

The *sense* of guilt won't usually change when the objective *fact* of guilt does. Like other natural consequences—pregnancy, for instance—feelings don't necessarily disappear when God transforms your life. But their sting is taken away.

Jesus didn't die on the cross to take away your feelings. He died to take away your sins. Cleansed of sin, you can work on transforming your feelings. They need not lead you downward. When you become transformed, they can give you a new compassion for others in their pain. And they can give you deep determination not to go wrong again.

People often grow impatient in this process because transforming your feelings takes time. They ask, "Will I ever get over it? Will I *ever* stop feeling this guilt and reliving those experiences?" The answer is yes—with time and in a healing environment you will. It may take longer than you dreamed it could, though. It's hard to overestimate the power of sexual experiences. They take a long time to fade from one's memory.

In a sense, that time is good for you. You're going through something like a grieving process. Normally you think of grieving when a loved one dies. But grieving for your lost innocence can be somewhat similar. It takes time to work through your emotions. You can't hurry the transformation of your feelings.

People try, though, in a variety of ways. They look for someone to "replace" the lost love. They move to a new school, a new town, a new job. They try praying harder or differently in the hope that God will perform special surgery on their memories. Often, those "hurry-up" techniques just make things worse. People rush into new experiences they're not emotionally ready to handle, and when problems arise, they drop even lower than they started. Love "on the rebound" is a classic example.

When you're in the recovery phase it's better to give yourself time and space. Let the wounds heal. If you have confidence that, in God's timing, he will renew you entirely, and you are wholly trusting in him, it's much easier to wait patiently.

You need a healing environment where you have the encouragment of friends and family who will pray for you, talk with you, and support you. If you're all alone with your memories, there's no guarantee that time will heal you. You may grow increasingly bitter—some do. People who have been wounded need others who will help them to find their courage again, who will help them feel the forgiving grace of Jesus by their deep, personal care.

I Can't Quit

Another kind of guilt is far more difficult. It's the guilt that gets renewed day by day because you're stuck in a sexual pattern you can't quit. In sexual matters, many people struggle with the dynamic Paul described in Romans: "I have the desire to do what is good, but I cannot carry it out. For what I do is not the good I want to do; no, the evil I do not want to do—this I keep on doing" (Romans 7:18-19).

I hate to think how many people I've known who can appreciate the meaning of Paul's words. They loathe themselves for what they can't stop doing—but loathing doesn't help them stop. Here's a typical example:

> *My fiancé and I are getting married in three months. Guilt surrounds us. We are trapped! We have not been pure, partly my doing. I forced him to comply with what I wanted. We can't go back. We have tried to quit, but to no avail. We have failed so many times! Who stays pure? Who can do it? I do not know of any of my Christian friends my age (twenty) who are still virgins.*

Sexually, people struggle with a law built into their biological make-up. It says: "Onward!" Couples go from holding hands to kissing to caressing to intercourse. They don't need a book to tell them what comes next. At every point, their bodies urge them on. The same law draws couples who've had sexual intercourse to have it again and again—even if they're determined to quit because they feel miserably guilty.

This law helps married couples, for even when they're out of sorts with each other, sexual attraction draws them together. Intercourse helps heal and restore their relationship. The power of sex is a bond between them.

But if you're not married, if your love hasn't grown to the point of commitment, and yet you've gone "all the way" with your bodies, you have a problem. Stopping sex isn't just a matter of making a decision. You have to fight off the laws of sex—something like fighting off gravity.

You can't fight gravity without some equipment—a set of wings and a motor. You can't fight sexual gravity, either, without some help. Generally this means: (1) Help from an outsider—a sympathetic Christian who will pray for you and to whom you will be accountable for your behavior; (2) Complete restructuring of your relationship.

You can't back up a step in sexual intimacy. You need a radical change. Here's the recipe I recommend if you truly want to quit:

- Eliminate meeting alone. You want to talk? Do it in a restaurant or a shopping mall.
- Go back to good-night kisses—brief ones and nothing more. Let your body get used to the joys of holding hands again.
- Spend your time with groups of people. If there's no ready-made group, like a school club or a church group, get your own together. Invite some friends along wherever you want to go.

- Don't drink alcohol or go to questionable movies. If you go to a concert or a party, make sure it's not a crazy one. Stay out of situations that encourage you to go back to your old ways.

It may not be a pleasant process. It will probably seem awkward, even childish. You'll miss those intimate, personal encounters, those whispered conversations. You'll miss the physical closeness. Meeting in public feels so impersonal. You'll wonder whether it's worth the pain.

Only those with determination to do what is right in spite of the pain will know that it's worth the cost to keep the dream alive.

It's far easier not to get involved sexually in the first place. It's far easier to keep sex under control than to try and bring it back under control. Yet it can be done. People have done it. They have risen from their failures to live the dream.

They discovered that conversations don't have to be whispered to be significant. They discovered that love doesn't depend on physical intimacy. Not that sexual attraction wasn't there any more. But they discovered that they loved each other's minds and personalities. When they kept sex under control, they found deeper reasons for loving each other. And even in the impersonal atmosphere of the public eye, they loved just being together.

Q: My boyfriend and I have been going out for over a year. We met when we were hanging around the same crowd. I'm eighteen and he's twenty-one. Now I have a five-month-old baby from him.

Here's my problem. When we met we used to go out and party together. (I'm a Christian, but I've been out of fellowship for about three years.) At that time I didn't know he was an alcoholic. Well, obviously now I know. I would like to get back with the Lord—I just feel so out of touch. I love Rick, but I know without the Lord I can never reach him. There's a part of me I've wanted to share with him for so long. He knows I'm a Christian, but that's all he knows.

Our relationship is going downhill because of his constant drinking and irresponsibility. As for me, I'm tired of the way I've been living. I want Jesus back in my life, but I feel so defeated and used up. I can feel the Lord calling me back. He's given me a beautiful child and a chance to start over and raise my daughter in the way he wants me to, but I don't know what to do.

Rick needs help with his drinking. And I need help spiritually. I can't witness to him till I get my own life straightened out. My situation is complicated, and I'm sure you know I'm only scratching the surface. If you have any advice from what I've told you, I'd really appreciate it.

A: Your situation is complicated indeed. You sound as weary as an old woman—it's hard to believe you're just eighteen. My advice is simple: You need help. You are not going to pull your life together on your own with the aid of a little advice from me. You need some Christians who will show concern for you, regularly check on you, and provide some experienced counseling for you and Rick. If I were you, I'd put all my available energy into finding such people. I wish every church in the phone book would give you what you need, but I'm afraid such people aren't that common. However, they do exist. Look for a Bible-believing church and start calling pastors. And don't quit until you find help.

I think this is the only way to get wisdom about how to handle Rick and your circumstances. Alcoholism, your daughter, Rick's attitude toward marriage—all these are factors that must be considered carefully and prayerfully.

What strikes me is the weariness and trouble that can enter a person's life in just one short year. I'm sure you just wanted to have fun. I doubt it ever occurred to you that you could feel so used up at eighteen. However, just as amazing is the renewal that can come into your life from the Lord. You want him back? I have good news for you—he wants you back, too.

Read in your Bible a story Jesus told: the Prodigal Son (Luke 15:11-32). Some people have said that the story was given the wrong name. Even though it focuses on a prodigal (lost) child, the center of the story is the father who waits for him to return. The story should be called, "The Waiting Father." Read how that father greeted his child. With reproaches? No. The father greeted his child with a bearhug and a party. That's the way the best fathers treat their children. And that's the way the best Father of all will treat you. ██

CHAPTER TWELVE

THE ART OF A HEALTHY RELATIONSHIP

A widespread myth says love is a natural thing. If you find the right lover (the one in a million who's right for you), you'll be happy. Find the person who sets you on fire, who inspires you, who excites you. That's the key to living the dream. *Find the right one.* Then do what comes naturally.

And so, with every potential partner you ask, "Is this the right one—the one with whom I can build a lifetime bond? Is this truly love?"

The problem is, how do you know who the right one is? Do you judge him or her just by your feelings? Or are there more rational guidelines?

Does my character have anything to do with it? If lasting love is just a question of matching "the right ones," then what is my part in forming a healthy, growing relationship?

It doesn't depend on a certain giddy feeling. It depends on character. It depends on work. It depends on patience. *It depends on prayer.*

The key question isn't really, "How do I find the right one?"

The key question is, "How do I build a right relationship?"

WHAT IS A GOOD RELATIONSHIP?

You need to know what a good relationship is. Try to forget what you learn from television or the movies. You may find some reality buried in a few unusual shows, but most of what TV teaches you about love is pure fantasy, dreamed up by people who belong on the No-Star team for crumbling relationships. Learning about love from TV is like learning self-defense from a Roadrunner cartoon.

Instead, observe your parents. Whether their marriage is good, bad, or indifferent, you'll see more reality there in ten minutes than you'd see in a month of movies.

If your parents have a good marriage, ask them some questions, such as: What made you decide to get married? What attracted you to each other? What qualities do you think are most important in keeping love alive and growing?

If your parents' marriage is bad, if they don't have a loving-caring relationship, look around for other couples—positive role models—and ask them questions. Everyone loves to share wisdom on this subject. How can you build a strong relationship if you've never studied one?

You also need positive ideas. What kind of person are you looking for? What qualities make love last? Try the library. Better yet, try a Christian bookstore. There is a ton of literature available.

What you'll learn, in general, is this: Building a lifetime relationship of love has little to do with good looks, popularity, or sex appeal. Even "in love" feelings, as good as they are, have their limits. A lifetime of love has more to do with trust, care, sacrifice, unselfishness, communication, patience, persistence, and reliability. A lifetime of love has a lot to do with your character and your partner's character.

BECOMING THE RIGHT PARTNER

Walter Trobisch, a wise counselor on love and sex, used to say that people worry too much about finding the right one. They ought to worry about *becoming* the right one.

Let's look at some specifics. They're not magical—you could meet these qualifications and still be a creep. But they usually make a difference.

Drinking and partying. People who get drunk, do drugs, and fool around in other ways make poor partners. Their chances of finding lasting love are small because they make such a poor contribution to their half of the relationship. They'll persistently avoid difficulties in favor of having what they call "a good time."

Surveys show a very strong correlation between kids who are sexually active and kids who drink. This probably is because of the partying scene more than the alcohol. But alcohol has destroyed many lives and wrecked many homes. I've heard from a number of people who woke up the next morning with no memory of what they did—but with the awful sense of certainty that something had been done to them. One girl

described it this way: "I don't remember anything after the fourth beer,
yet when I got home in the morning I was without a bra, and my under-
wear was inside out. I know in my heart that mentally I'm still a virgin,
but I'm no longer one physically." Think about it. That's an awful memory to live with.

Studying. Surveys also show that people who do well in school—
who study hard, who work hard, who are conscientious—generally
make good partners. Not that you should pick out a partner by his grade-
point average, but you could certainly think about what *your* grade-point
average says about you. And when you're looking for love, keep in
mind the character traits that a grade-point average can indicate. People
who are willing to work to achieve good grades often make strong marriages because they are willing to work at achieving good relationships.

Faith. Those who have a strong faith in God and who live that faith
out in practical ways (including such ordinary ways as going to church),
often have the stability and the idealism needed to make strong relationships. Jesus challenged his followers to love each other sacrificially.
Such love is the foundation of all good relationships. If you want a good
partner, look in church. If you want to *become* a good partner, go to
church.

If you add these qualities together, what do you get? Somebody who
doesn't get drunk, do drugs, or carouse, who works hard in school and
gets good grades, who attends church regularly and sincerely practices
his faith.

Right there you see one reason why so many fail to live up to the
dream. We know what it takes to make love last, but unfortunately it's
commonly believed that people who have such qualities are dull.

Remember what I told you about forgetting what you've learned from
TV? Believe me, there is nothing dull about being in love for a lifetime.

AT LAST—THE RELATIONSHIP

If you've got your thinking straight, and you've got your life-style on
track, you're ready to think about The Relationship. Relationships are a
test of character. Do you have what it takes to love this person for the rest
of your life? Does he have what it takes to love you for the rest of your
life? Obviously, these aren't easy questions to answer.

You can be fairly accurate, however, about The Wrong One. First on
the list of Wrong Ones are sexual predators. To them, sex is just something people do without commitment. They're often very attractive peo-

ple. But they're deadly. If you're serious about love that lasts, steer away from them. That means pay attention to reputations. No matter how nice they seem, how cute they look, or how much they attract you—if they've used other people, they're likely to use you, too.

Talk, Talk, Talk

You learn about people by talking, more than by any other way. For some people that's natural—they talk, talk, talk, all the time. Others, however, are so shy they can hardly put one word in front of another. But even for shy people, communication is crucial. Only by communicating can you discover what's going on inside someone you think you like.

The person who talks a lot may need to slow down and perhaps listen more in order to genuinely communicate. The shy person on the other hand, needs to summon up the courage to say at least a few words. But each couple can find their own style. Shyness isn't an insurmountable problem.

You need to observe, too. It's good to see how a boyfriend's father and mother treat each other, for he will most likely emulate that behavior later on. It's also been said that if you want to know how a girl will treat you after you're married, you should visit her home and see how she treats her little brother. That's meant to be a joke, but there is some truth to it. Watch your friend in all kinds of situations—particularly under pressures of home or school. You'll learn a lot about his or her character.

GOOD COMMUNICATION

Bringing two unique people together in a close relationship requires that they try to understand each other—that takes communication. Great feelings, comfortable silences, having fun together—these are no substitutes for communication.

Few people are naturally good communicators. Communication is not the same as talking a lot. It has more to do with listening carefully. You must explore new ground, not just talk about the things you've been doing or the latest gossip circulating among your friends. Communication requires that you put into words the ideas, beliefs, and feelings that make you a unique personality, but which your partner may not share. Communication is, therefore, hard work.

First, here's what not to do. When two people can't find anything to say, they're tempted to fill in the silence by getting physical. While making out does cover the embarrassment and even leaves a feeling of becoming closer, it never substitutes for communication. If you try to make it a substitute, you will wreck your relationship.

So, how do you learn to communicate? There is no magic formula, only practice, practice, practice. As in learning basketball, you feel awkward at first. You just have to keep practicing until it begins to feel smooth. Here are a few hints that might help you:

1. Keep your practice sessions short and frequent. It's much better to have an in-depth conversation every day for five minutes than to have a superficial talk once a week for two hours.

2. Carry a notebook and jot down thoughts you'd like to communicate so that your partner can understand you better. Keep track of feelings, opinions, conversations that come up in the events of the day. Then, when you talk, just go through the list. Get your partner to do the same.

3. Learn to ask questions and follow-up questions. You can jot these down in your notebook. "What did you do today?" is a poor question. "How does the basketball coach act in practice?" or "What is it about basketball that you like?" are better questions.

4. Share spiritually by telling each other what the Lord is teaching you from your personal study of the Bible (no matter how small). Pray with and for each other about specific activities or problems you may have. Then you will not be talking just for the sake of talking. You'll be communicating in order to help as well as to understand. ███

THE LONELY COUPLE

When you're in love, you crave privacy. You want to make the world go away. This is natural. To a point, it's good. If you're serious about your relationship, you need time together, without distractions.

But you also need to live normal lives. A healthy couple touches the world around them. They

- enjoy the company of mutual friends;
- talk to others about their problems, their hopes, their dreams;
- like to be around each other's family;
- don't feel persecuted when their time together is interrupted;
- work together to get a job done—to make cookies or to clean house or to help a friend.

The difference between a lonely couple and a healthy couple has to do with purpose. For what reason, fundamentally, are they spending time together? For fun? For romance? To check each other out as potential marriage partners? A healthy couple would add another purpose, which stays strong even when romance goes out the window: "To spur each other on toward love and good deeds," as the Bible puts it in Hebrews 10:24.

Even if you discover you aren't right for each other—if you don't see the possibility of a lifetime commitment—the relationship ought not to be wasted time. A healthy couple aims to leave each other better off than they found each other. They aim to learn lessons, together, in how to love, so that sweetness and pleasant memories endure. They aim to leave each other better people, without bitter memories and unhealed wounds.

To do that, they must get to know each other at a deeper level. They must learn each other's dreams and fears. They must gain an understanding of each other's deepest needs. Knowing these things, and understanding each other, they must care for each other. By care, I mean: look after, look out for, shelter, serve, cherish, and love.

SEX UNDER CONTROL

A healthy relationship doesn't ignore the sexual wiring. It's to be appreciated and watched as much as the weather.

Appreciation requires that you thank God for your life as a male or a female—and thank God for the differences.

Appreciation requires that you look forward with excitement to your wedding day when you can begin a life of unrestrained, unending sexual expression.

Watching requires that you think through how to handle this power in your present relationship. You see how important it is and how powerful, and you monitor it closely to see that it doesn't overwhelm you.

Here are some guidelines to follow to avoid any tug-of-wars about sex:

■ *The person with the most sensitive conscience should automatically prevail, without argument.* Nobody should ever have to compromise on his or her sense of what's right.
■ *Limits should be set and clearly defined ahead of time.* Awkward as it may be, talk about specifics. This doesn't mean you must talk about

all your experiences and lay out your total philosophy on the first date. It just means you should talk before the situation is out of control.

For instance, setting the limit as "kissing" may seem safe, but if you spend three hours "just kissing," that's hardly balanced or healthy. And if you spend three hours after dark kissing in a parked car, you are asking for trouble.

■ *Don't push the limits.* Some couples draw a line and then spend all their time leaning over it. Don't push the limits of your endurance to the point that you have to say, "We just couldn't help ourselves." Concentrate your energy on enjoying each other, not on wringing the maximum sexual stimulation from every activity you've agreed on.

WHY DATE?

Q: Is God ever glorified in a romantic relationship other than marriage? Is there any reason to consider dating when you are not ready to consider marriage?

A: I think so. Members of the opposite sex do not merely relate to each other "in ministry." There is considerable art in learning how to understand each other in a dating context. Dating offers a good opportunity to learn. Over a period of time you can begin to understand the opposite sex a little, and you can also ease some of the loneliness that afflicts us all. ■■

WHERE DO WE DRAW THE LINE?

One of the limits which the Bible clearly sets is on sexual intercourse: Sex is for married people only.

Many people who want to honor and obey God in this regard wonder how far they can go and still not go "all the way." What's right and what's wrong? And where do you draw the line?

Since the Bible doesn't give explicit details, it's up to us to form a realistic view based on what we know is right. Several principles apply:

- *You should do only what is helpful for your relationship.* You don't draw the line just by claiming, "There's nothing wrong with it." What you should do is ask, "What's right about it?" For kissing and hugging to be right they should genuinely express love and appreciation. A realistic question would be, "Just how far do you need to go to show your love and appreciation?"

- *You should stay away from activities that create more frustration than appreciation.* Whenever two people of the opposite sex touch each other in a loving way, they enter a track designed to lead to intercourse. What is called "petting" outside of marriage is referred to as "foreplay" within marriage. It's lovely, exciting touching that prepares the way for the joy of sex.

  But when you don't go all the way, it's considerably less lovely. Our bodies weren't designed to stop halfway. The further along this track you go, the more frustrating it is to stop. It's hard on people to get all steamed up and then quit. They can end the evening feeling hot, angry, and unfulfilled. That, surely, isn't the best.

- *Physical interactions shouldn't dominate the relationship.* You only have so many hours together, and if you're spending a good portion of those hours in silence making out, you're not really getting closer—no matter how close it makes you feel.

- *You should keep private parts private.* Sexual intercourse is a symbolic expression of total unity between two married people for they are "naked and unashamed." That kind of psychological and physical nakedness is meant only for married people, not for unmarried people. When people start touching parts normally covered, they are straying into a territory God reserved for married people.

It's hard to bring all these principles into one practical definition of how far to go. It's surely different for different people. What's stimulating for one person may seem tame to another. Also, "how far to go" will depend on where you are in your relationship. On your first date you will have different considerations than a couple who have been going together for a year. You need to match your physical expressions to the length of time you have known each other and to the depth of your commitment. You also need to commit this area of your lives to God—giving your bodies as a living sacrifice to him (Romans 12:1).

It is my conviction, based on the experiences of many people who have shared with me, that it's a good idea to stick just to holding hands or kissing on dates. Touching parts of the body that are private, including breasts and thighs, generates sexual excitement that is hard to contain and leads only to frustration. God intended this to be part of the act of love—a joyful, fulfilling experience for married people only.

PETTING?

Q: Is petting off limits?

A: Let's start with a definition. *Petting* may mean:
   a. Hugging so that your hands caress your partner's back and sides.
   b. Touching breasts and groin through clothing.
   c. Touching breasts and groin under the clothing.
   d. Lying down next to each other or on top of each other.
   e. Touching sexual organs.
   f.   Touching sexual organs in order to reach orgasm.

When you wonder whether petting is a sin, the first thing to do is look in the Bible. However, the Bible says nothing directly about whether any of these activities is right or wrong outside of marriage. It does emphasize, though, that God intended marriage as the secure, loving environment where a husband and wife could enjoy their sexuality. People in biblical times would have recognized any of the activities on this list as being preliminary to sexual intercourse and experienced within marriage.

The question is this: Should a couple who love each other enjoy some of these preliminaries of lovemaking while "stopping short" of going all the way? The preliminaries feel good and yet don't lead to pregnancies, herpes, AIDS, etc. So is it only sexual intercourse that is off limits for unmarried people? Is there some line short of intercourse where we ought to stop?

I think there is. The Bible doesn't guide us directly, and it's possible for Christians to have various viewpoints. Here are my conclusions. Whether you agree or disagree with them, I hope you'll consider them seriously and use them to arrive at some definite standards of your own.

Too often couples work backwards—they try something out, then consider whether it's right or not. That's a recipe for rationalization. It's better to determine in advance what is right for you as a Christian and stick to it.

I rule out two extremes from the beginning. On the one hand, I disagree with those Christians who think that couples should treat each other as "brother and sister" until they are married. That's an imaginary world, and I think we should live in the real world. People of the opposite sex feel romantically attracted to each other and have no reason to be embarrassed by that fact. It's good, because God made us that way. I believe that communicating the attraction to each other is OK, if it is done with genuine concern to protect each other from harm. When people try to pretend the feelings aren't there, they often end up with phony relationships.

On the other hand, I disagree with those who make virginity a technicality. Such people say that so long as two people don't actually have sexual intercourse they are all right. I say that God's concern for virginity is not a matter of anatomy but of privacy. He wants people to reserve some "private parts" for their married partner alone. Only in marriage ought two people be naked and unashamed, as Adam and Eve were. When two people touch each other's sexual organs, I believe they are doing what is appropriate for married people alone. Therefore, *e* and *f* on my list are out of bounds.

I would also put *b, c,* and *d* out of bounds. They're not as intimate as touching sexual organs, yet I think they are more harmful than helpful to a relationship. Here are my reasons for thinking so:

1. They cause frustration. The further you go, the harder stopping becomes. I have yet to hear that frustration is helpful to a relationship.

2. Petting feels good, but it will not continue to feel as good as it does. Gradually it will become more frustrating than fulfilling. It's a general rule of the book. Holding hands gives a tremendous thrill the first time, but eventually it just gives sweat. Kissing has atomic power early on but becomes quite routine. The same is true of all forms of petting. After a while, they don't thrill the way they did. The body wants to go on and won't settle down at any level short of going all the way. Therefore, any beautiful feelings tend to be short term. And you want whatever builds a good long-term relationship.

3. Touching leads to other things. It doesn't have to, but it is hard to stop and keep stopping over months or perhaps years of dating. When you're fifteen and talking about marriage, you're looking at the possibility of three to seven years of stopping. It's a long time to wait. You're more likely to succeed if you set limits you can easily live with—rather than stimulating "beautiful feelings" so you will constantly think of going on.

4. These areas of the body are private. They are not as private as the sexual organs, but they represent a degree of intimacy which is out of place between two people who are just going together.

Where do you draw the line, then? That's probably different for different cultures. Conservative Muslims are convinced that even *seeing* each other is too provocative. They would look on kissing as completely decadent. In our culture, I think most people can handle kissing and hugging, especially if they don't do it for too long at a time. (If you kiss for more than ten minutes at a time, you're either looking for trouble, or you're trying to wear out your lips. A fifteen-minute kiss does not communicate more love and tenderness than a two-minute kiss. It just communicates more desire.)

Kissing and hugging are not "second rate" in any way. They can express beautiful, romantic feelings and genuine love. In some ways they make a far warmer, more personable demonstration of love than petting does, for they are not so charged with urgent sexual desires.

There is one more question, which I am sure many people want to ask: How do we stop doing what we've enjoyed doing so much? I can assure you that it is not easy to do. Most people think they've got their sexuality well under control until they try not doing something they've become accustomed to doing. Then they discover the power of sex as an element of life humans find hard to control.

The only effective way to stop is to start over. Don't try to back up your physical intimacy just one notch. Either break off entirely or start as though you only just met, but keep it very formal physically—with no involvement at all. At first this will feel very awkward. But you need to get your body back to the point where it finds holding hands an incredible privilege—which, indeed, it is. ■■

CHAPTER THIRTEEN

FINDING THE RIGHT ONE

In the dream, you love a particular someone—the right one. But what if you make a mistake? The dream could turn into a nightmare—the horror of being caught in a commitment to the wrong person. That became a nightmare of a friend of mine.

He had the jitters. Recently out of college, he was due to be married in a few weeks. Now he was wondering whether he should go through with it. His fiancée was beautiful and talented, but suddenly he did not find her physically attractive. He dared not tell her his feelings, since he was sure they would only hurt and confuse her. He felt tremendous internal turmoil. As a Christian, he believed that marriage was for life; he did not intend to just try it on for size. But how should he interpret his jitters? Did they indicate some fundamental flaw in his relationship to his fiancée? Was God sending him a message through them? Or were these merely predictable prewedding doubts?

He talked this over with my wife, a trained counselor. She went into some depth with him, but could detect nothing fundamentally wrong with his relationship with his fiancée. Still, the final decision whether or not to marry was up to him; no one could make it for him.

He finally did decide to marry the girl. The wedding came off on schedule. Evidently, it was the right decision. He and his wife have been happily married for over ten years, they have several children, and I am sure their friends view them as a model couple. Everything worked out for the best. Looking back, it seems clear that our friend *did* merely suffer from a case of prewedding jitters.

Unfortunately, some people have a very different experience. I recall a quiet young woman whom I got to know while riding the bus to work. She was always rather distant until one day when she spilled out the story of her recent marriage.

As her wedding day approached and gifts piled up in her parents' home, she had increasing doubts about whether she was doing the right thing. Everyone thought the world of her fiancé; they thought she was making a prize catch. But was she? She wasn't sure. Yet she said nothing. Everyone was counting on her, and she wouldn't dream of spoiling the plans by changing her mind. *Somehow,* she thought, *everything will work out.*

The wedding went as scheduled, and they traveled to Paris for their honeymoon. However, while they were there she had something close to a nervous breakdown because of her husband's mistreatment. She could foggily remember seeing the beautiful Parisian streets, but only through her constant tears. Her new husband was far from understanding, and her worst fears became a reality. She flew home, had the wedding annulled, and left her home town to live quietly with an aunt, trying to recover the broken pieces of her life. That was when I met her. In her case, everything had not worked out for the best. It had worked out into a nightmare.

WHO IS "THE RIGHT ONE"?

The question of "the right one" comes particularly strongly to those who do not believe in divorce—who want to marry once, for life. If they have doubts, how can they resolve them? How can they know for sure that they have found the right one? Even when a person isn't considering marriage, when he meets someone for the first time the question may cross his mind: Is this the right one?

Out of all the hundreds of people of the opposite sex whom you meet, how will you know the right one? Will some sixth sense tell you? Will you "just know," as some say? Will you feel internal shivers? Or will some rational analysis, using computer matching or values clarification, make the right one obvious?

From a strictly human point of view, the very idea that out of several billion individuals on this planet there is only one person—the right one—suited to you is nonsense. Even if there were just one person, how could you be confident of finding him or her?

If you lived for eighty years as an extraordinarily outgoing person, and each day you met 100 new persons, you would meet in your lifetime a grand total of 2,922,000 people—less than one tenth of one percent of the world's population. On the basis of this tiny sampling, how could you possibly claim you have found "the right one"?

Yet it is my belief that if God has called you to be married, he does have just one person for you. I believe that you can be absolutely certain of finding him or her by walking in the light of God. And you will be able to say for certain, "This woman [or this man] is the only one for me."

Not all Christians see it just this way. Some would say God doesn't have one particular person picked out for you. They would say you might marry any one of a number of people. Perhaps they are right. Profound issues arise when you try to understand exactly how God guides our lives while respecting our freedom.

Without being dogmatic, however, I will stick to my belief that each person can ultimately discover the right one to marry. I believe in the right one partly because of my own marriage experience. I still marvel that God so lovingly gave my wife to me—not just one of several possibilities, but this particular flesh-and-blood person whom I love so deeply. She is unique, and, I believe, uniquely right for me. Perhaps I could have had a good marriage with another woman, but it would not have been the same.

The Woman of My Dreams

I was a painfully shy kid who went out with only a handful of girls in high school and college. After college graduation I moved from my California home to Illinois, where I took my first job. I lived in the Chicago suburbs for the next five years. I was happily single. Like most single people, though, I did want to marry. I went out with several girls whom I liked very much. Yet I never became deeply serious. Why? I was not sure myself.

During that same period I met Popie. She lived in California, and I met her through some old school friends when I visited there. I liked her very much, though to the casual eye we were opposites. I was shy and serious, and she was extremely outgoing and lighthearted. I never gave serious thought to romantic involvement with her.

Frankly, she seemed out of my reach. Plenty of guys were jostling to get her attention. Besides, I lived two thousand miles away and was rather naive about dating. How could I compete? I looked at her the way you might look at the big white mansion on the hill. Of course, it would be nice to live in a mansion like that, but I didn't expect to do so. And I didn't expect to marry Popie.

Then a terrrible thing happened. After I had known her for several years, I fell in love with her. I had not intended to do so, but love came without asking my permission. It came when she visited me while passing through the midwest one summer. Nothing like it had troubled me since the sixth grade. I became intoxicated with love and could only think about her. This was intensely annoying to me because I was almost sure that she was not interested in me. I did not fancy myself as becoming one of the droves of males unsuccessfully pursuing her. I was too proud.

I thought the feeling would pass, as hopeless infatuations usually do. It didn't. I wrote her a letter to see whether she was interested in romance with me and waited anxiously for her response. She said, nicely, that she was not interested. Still the feeling didn't pass. Months later it was still with me, an oversweet sickness in my gut. I wanted very much to stop feeling it, but I couldn't. I looked at other girls whom I knew and admired, girls who I thought *were* interested in romance with me. I wished I could feel the same way toward them that I felt toward Popie. I couldn't.

So over the next year I tried to proudly stifle my feelings for her. Two or three times they broke into the open. I would tell her what I felt and ask her whether she felt any differently. Each time I hoped, desperately, that she would have changed her mind. She had not. My heart actually hurt. Until that time I had not known that the phrase "a broken heart" was based on a physical sensation.

I could not understand why I was going through such an experience. I still do not understand. I know that through it I came to a far deeper understanding of God's love for me—a love undimmed by hard and confusing times. I know, too, that one unforgettable day, when I had given up all hope, Popie told me she had changed her mind. She was "open," she said. The doors of my heart, at this word, yawned apart. In a year's time we were married. I have never doubted that she was uniquely meant for me—a gift from God's hand.

Many married people feel this way about their partners. Even in marriages which have been quite difficult, the partners may have a profound sense that they were meant for each other. One man told me, "We have plenty of days when both of us wish we were married to someone else. Yet we both feel that God meant us specifically for each other. Even the hard parts of our marriage work to make us better people."

I think this feeling matches the Bible's feeling about life. For me as a Christian, God is not an abstract force. He is my personal Father. He knows how many hairs are on my head. I may not know the 4 billion human beings on the surface of this planet, but he does. He pays very personal attention to each one. Not even a sparrow falls without his notice. Such a heavenly father shows interest in the most petty details of my life. I believe nothing happens by accident.

Certainly marriages don't, for he has expressed his deep concern for marriages. They are used in the Bible as an analogy of God's love for us (see Ephesians 5:22-33). Believing in such a God, and believing that he has adopted me into his family, how could I think that the choice of whom to marry is no matter for God's concern? It may be that God has no concern for whether I put on a blue or red shirt in the morning, but how could he not care about whom I marry?

I can't prove that God has a right one picked out for each person. The Bible doesn't say that. I merely assert that the belief in "the right one" is almost inevitable for Christians. We do not think of our lives as made up of arbitrary choices. Rather, we believe they follow or are a result of the will of God. Inevitably, as Christians we cling to the sense that our situations are not arbitrary, but they are God's specific will for us.

My belief is that God has one particular woman to be my wife, just as he has one particular job for me to work at, and one particular town for me to live in, and particular river for each fish to swim in. He didn't make a million different possible universes. He made one universe—the right one. It may be a difficult universe, a universe filled with pain as well as joy. But it is not out of control. It is God's universe. Everything is directed by his care.

But this is quite philosophical. The Bible is a practical book, concerned with what you need to know for living. Even if the right one exists, you have to find him or her. In practice, this turns out to be quite difficult.

Some Theories on the Choice

Some people will tell you, "You just *know* when the right person comes along," and often you do. The right person may "click" for you, like the right answer to a mathematical problem you've been trying to solve. This was the case with me. I never suffered from a moment's doubt that if this wonderful creature was willing to marry me, she was the right one. You could say that her willingness alone was miraculous proof of God's will.

Yet that perfect fit may prove deceptive. No one knows himself perfectly. That's why you find so many people changing majors in college, or changing careers after college. What you thought you'd like you often don't. And where love is concerned, you are particularly vulnerable. Every cell in your body urges you on. You can fool yourself because you want to be fooled; you may marry your "dream love" and become utterly miserable.

Do you think those millions who march down the aisle each spring think they are marrying the right one? Of course they do. Half of them, unfortunately, change their minds within a year or two. They ultimately divorce, feeling bitterness and hatred for the one they called "the right one." Their dream has dissolved.

Christians try to be a degree smarter. Knowing the dangers in living by their emotions, they turn to God for wisdom. Through prayer they search for the right one. I've heard people say, "The Lord showed me that she [or he] is the right one for me to marry." But don't press them too hard on how the Lord showed them, or you'll find (usually, at least) that the Lord was using very subjective means to get his message across: feelings, impressions, a sense of peace. Feelings or impressions are not as reliable as people pretend. A sense of peace may say more about your own state of mind than God's—an important concern when you're making an important decision. You can get a sense of peace with Valium, too. There's no verse in the Bible promising that inner peace is a reliable guide to God's will.

In the Bible you find people guided by visions, voices from heaven, and other supernatural means (not feelings). But even in the Bible such supernatural intervention is not the only means of guidance. Decisions often were based on an understanding of what God cares about as revealed in Scripture, and on common sense. This is still the case today. Most missionaries go overseas because they have a deep interest in spreading the gospel, not because an angel appeared to them. Most Christians marry because they are in love, not because they heard "a voice." A lot of people have asked God to show his will, but very few of them have claimed to see visions or to hear actual voices in response. Most are left to use more ordinary criteria for making a decision. And, using ordinary criteria, you cannot achieve absolute certainty that a certain girl sitting three rows in front of you is the right one for you.

God Reveals "The Right One"

You don't know everything about your potential partner. You don't know lots of things about yourself. You can't begin to guess the future.

You may marry a beauty today, and the next week a car accident may smash her pretty face. You may marry a strong, stable and self-confident man today, and tomorrow he may lose his job and fall into a deep depression. You may marry thinking you will have children and then discover you can't have any. You may marry thinking of sexual intimacy and then discover that you both have terrible sexual hangups. (This surprise, by the way, comes to those who experiment with premarital sex as well as those who don't—for the simple reason that premarital sex is not the same as married sex.)

So even if you believe there is a right one, what good does that do you? How can you know for sure who it is?

The answer I'm going to give—it's the Bible's, I believe—may frustrate you. As is so often the case with the Bible, it doesn't solve your problem the way you wanted it solved. Here is its answer: *You know the right one for sure on the day you stand in front of a preacher and say "I do."* Until that day you probably won't know for sure. After that day the issue is settled, forever.

I told you the answer might frustrate you. It seems like a trick. You want to know the right one in order to make the choice simple. Instead, the choice becomes more demanding. You make the choice on your own, and then when you've made it you hear the door locking behind you. Your choice has suddenly become God's choice.

I believe we find this frustrating because we don't want to face the difficult facts about marriage—and about ourselves. We want to reduce marriage mainly to a question of finding the right combination of personalities, like finding the right key for a lock. We hold potential partners up against a list of ideal qualities to see how they rate.

I certainly believe that compatibility is important. However, it is not the most important criterion in a successful marriage. God's main focus is not compatibility, but a question which cuts to the heart of marriage: *Can you say "I do" and stick with it until death?* If you can, then you have *found* "the right one"—and you have also *become* "the right one."

Do we see so much divorce, unhappiness, suicide, wife and child abuse, and promiscuity because, through a mental mistake, millions of Americans found the wrong person? No. We want to blame our problems on "mistakes," preferably mistakes that no one could sensibly foresee. We can't bear to think of the alternative: Things go awry because we are wrong inside, because we can't take the pressures of life, because we can't above all love and keep loving in the way that happy living demands.

God makes hard questions bore into you as you think about marriage.

They are primarily questions about you, not your partner. Can you take the heat? Can you make the commitment and stick to it? God wants you to ask not only, "Is this the right person for me?" but. "Am *I* the right person?" In his way of thinking, compatibility is always secondary to commitment.

From the day you make those marriage vows, your question about the right person is answered. He or she is the right person for you to stick with, love, cherish. He or she may not prove to be the right person to make you happy, but he or she is certainly the right person to shape you—in better or worse conditions, in sickness or in health, in poverty or in wealth—into the person God wants you to become.

Holding Your Partner Up to a List

While more than a little frustrating, this answer does respond to our questions. It says, first of all, that there is a right one for you if you are called to marriage. This is more than saying that you have to make the best of a bad situation or that divorce is never a good option for a Christian. It says that God himself puts his stamp of approval on your marriage. He says that the one you make your marriage vows to is his perfect will for your life—no if's, and's, or but's. There is no such thing as second best in his thinking. There is no "might have been." He only urges you forward into the wonderful future he prepares for each of us. You can, therefore—in fact you will—find the right one. You will find yourself married to the one man or woman with whom God wants you to find marital fulfillment.

You even know how to find the right one. You find him or her by marrying. You have a grave responsibility for making the choice. In making that choice, you are finding God's will for you.

Does this imply that you cannot make a mistake? Does it mean, in the extreme, that a Christian could marry a non-Christian knowing full well that this violates 2 Corinthians 6:14 and yet find himself perfectly within God's will? No, disobedience to God is always a mistake. It will get you loads of unhappiness and trouble. So, for that matter, will a poor choice of a partner.

Yet in another sense the answer is yes. Because of his great love for marriage, God can take even rebellious or foolish marriages and still work through them. This is Paul's explicit comment to the Corinthians, who wondered whether mixed marriages should be dissolved. (These people had probably married when both were non-Christians, and then one was converted.) He wrote, "If any brother has a wife who is not a believer and she is willing to live with him, he must not divorce her. And if a woman has a husband who is not a believer and he is willing to live with her, she must not divorce him. *For the unbelieving husband has been sanctified through his wife, and the unbelieving wife has been sanctified through her believing husband"* (1 Corinthians 7:12-14). The word *sanctified* means "made holy," or "set apart for God's work." For Paul, there is no hopeless marriage. He doesn't imply that non-Christians are automatically made into Christians through marriage; they are not. He doesn't imply that a Christian partner who disobeyed God would pay no penalty for his or her disobedience; he or she will pay a penalty. What Paul does imply is that God is willing to make a marriage into what it would not otherwise be: a vehicle for his best.

So may a Christian marry a non-Christian or make some other unwise marriage plans? Not at all! How, in the first place, could a real Christian wish to disobey God and marry a non-Christian? Or why would a Christian want to enter marriage—which God has given as such a wonderful gift—with unwise or hasty plans? Marriage ought to be treated with reverent care, for that is how God treats it. Any other attitude can only lead you and your partner into the risk of great pain. Any other attitude would suggest that you are no more ready for marriage than a two-year-old is ready to defuse a delicate and complex time bomb.

Marriage should be entered into with all the wisdom you can muster. This is why you should make a list and see how your potential partner measures up. The proper purpose of the list—and I am going to give you a list—is to help you think about the commitment you are preparing to make. You want to be as sure as possible you are making it wisely and will live with it happily, since marriage is not an experiment but an absolute commitment in God's sight. You want to be sure you *can* live with it and *want* to live with it. A list of qualities, properly used, helps you make that commitment with confidence and wisdom.

There is no perfect partner. You are not perfect and neither will the right one be perfect. No matter whom you choose, you will have unhappy days. But you need to make a wise decision in order to find a partner who will give you joy and fellowship, who will join you in serving God. So you look for someone who fits you. You test, and think, and pray, and talk, until conviction comes that you have found the person God intended for you.

CHAPTER FOURTEEN

TWENTY QUESTIONS FOR CHOOSING "THE RIGHT ONE"

1. *Do you help each other grow closer to God?* For this to happen, you both must first have a relationship to God. This means that you have done more than just hang around a church. It means that you both talk to God, you care about his Word, and you have put God first in your lives. Good partners help each other grow in this relationship. A healthy relationship has a specifically spiritual dimension to it, one not just assumed.

Second, you should be able to encourage each other in fellowship with other Christians. At a purely practical level, you ought to be able to agree on a church to join. In practice, loving Jesus means loving his people and meeting with them regularly in some particular place to worship him. If you can't agree on a church, you're always going to be pulling in different directions rather than pulling together.

Third, you ought to be at approximately the same level of spiritual maturity. "Maturity" is hard to grade, but you know it when you see it. It's not intensity, but depth and consistency. Maturity comes as you learn to walk by the Spirit and as the Spirit produces increasing fruit in your life (as described in Galatians 5:22-23). If you're not sure how mature you and your partner are, ask your pastor or some older Christian whose judgment you trust. A marriage should be mutual: you should encourage each other to grow nearer to God. If one of you is far more mature than the other, the encouragement will grow one-sided.

2. *Can you talk?* Marriages aren't built on good looks but on good communication. The most crucial question you can ask about a potential partner is, Do we know how to communicate?

Can you talk about any subject you're interested in? Or are you re-stricted to talking about "us" or "me"? Talking about your marvelous love affair won't keep that marvelous love affair going. Talking about how wonderful one or both of you are will get old—especially when one or both of you doesn't seem so wonderful any longer. You need to be able to talk about other things.

It's true that some people are much bigger talkers than others. Quiet people may not say too many words in a day. There's nothing wrong with that. Communication can go at any speed you're both comfortable with, so long as there *is* communication. Don't settle for a comfortable feeling as a substitute. The mysterious attraction that doesn't need words grows even more mysterious after the wedding. But the mystery be-comes, *Why was I ever attracted to him/her? We have nothing to say to each other.*

3. *Can you play together?* Life isn't all talk. A couple needs to be able to help each other relax, laugh, and have fun. If you can't do it, the heavy, heart-thumping seriousness of your love will wear out. Love without laughter is like bread without yeast: it doesn't rise. It may smell heavenly but it turns out heavy and sticky.

4. *Can you work together?* Christian marriage is not merely an associ-ation for pleasure. It involves work. This comes naturally with living to-gether. Somebody has to cook, clean, wash clothes, rake leaves. If everyday chores aren't shared, then your life isn't shared; you aren't really "one" as you ought to be.

For most couples this shared work grows far more intense when they have children. Kids take work—unrewarded and often unpleasant work. You win no trophies and get no paychecks for cheerfully changing dirty diapers. But it has to be done. Marriage involves servanthood—service toward your children and family.

A Christian's basic orientation is bent this way: In helping others we find true happiness. In fact, we must die to ourselves if we are to find true life. Fulfillment is found as we put the welfare of others high on the list. We look for ways to serve our friends and neighbors—even when we don't feel like it.

How can you test these "thoroughly married" qualities while you are just going together? You can begin to look for ways to do things for oth-ers as a couple, and you can take up activities which involve more than eating food and watching movies. Can you clean a house together for someone who needs the help? Can you plan a party together? Can you both help in the church nursery? Can you get routine, unpleasant tasks done as a team?

5. *Do you have mutual friends?* You aren't going to spend all your lives with just each other. You will need other friends. It's important they are friends who don't split you apart but bring you together.

Observe the way your love gets along with his or her friends. Would *you* care to be one of them? Do you like the way he (or she) acts with others? More likely than not the way your partner treats friends is just how you will be treated after the wedding. Marriage isn't always terribly romantic. It's a friendship—or ought to be.

If you both enjoy the same people, it's a good sign of compatibility. If you don't like the same people, you should at least *get along* with the same people. A person who treats his or her partner's friends with contempt or total disinterest is not usually the easiest person to live with.

6. *Are you proud of each other?* You need privacy to get acquainted, but fairly often couples in love become like a space satellite orbiting planet earth. They are in their own world. This is quite unrealistic. Marriage involves lots of others: friends, ex-boyfriends and ex-girlfriends, parents, pastors, neighbors, even enemies. You don't have to be on intimate terms with all of these. But you do need to be proud of your partner in front of all these. A love that has no public strength is unlikely to endure.

Some people, it's true, love their partners *only* in front of the public. They display him or her like a fisherman showing off a fish. "Look what I got," they seem to say. Sometimes they do this to make a point to an old flame or to a rival. This won't do either. You must love your partner first for what he (or she) means to you privately; you should also love your partner for the effect he (or she) makes on others. You should be proud of your partner in private *and* in public.

7. *Are you intellectually on the same level?* Most of the time this goes with education. There are plenty of exceptions, but as a rule two people ought to have similar educational backgrounds.

In our society, education says a lot about who you are and what you enjoy. Two people may not use much of their education in ordinary conversation. Most people don't talk about books or discuss algebraic equations. However, their education will affect how they approach a problem, how they raise their children, how they balance a checkbook, and what kind of friends they naturally gravitate toward. Educational level is a rough but sturdy measure of intellectual level. There are exceptions, of course. Someone with a high school education may be more intellectual than another person with a master's degree. It happens—but not very often.

8. *Do you have common interests?* Beyond "us" that is. Common interests are the raw material for friendship. If one of you lives for sports and

the other grows nauseous at the sight of a football, you will need to make major adjustments to each other. It's better to be friends with someone who shares your interests so you have something to talk about together, and so that there will be things you like to do together.

The key word is *interest*. You can cultivate an interest. You can "take an interest" in a subject you never knew existed. You may not start out with much in common, but are you willing to work together at something?

9. *Do you share the same values?* About, for instance, being honest in "the little things" like income taxes? About the importance of a clean house and car? About the value of going to church every week? About the roles of men and women in marriage? About abortion? Divorce?

You don't need to have the same *opinions* on every subject. You don't have to vote for the same presidential candidate, or like the same kind of furniture, or root for the same team. (Though shared opinions do help smooth the way.) I'm talking about *values*, which deal with the meaning behind the facts. If you don't share values, you have no basis for a meaningful resolution of differences. You can't agree on where to live if one of you values a large house as a sign of God's blessing and the other considers it a sign of greed.

10. *Do you feel comfortable about how you make decisions together?* Most people use a certain way to arrive at a decision—probably because their parents operated that way. For instance, one person may feel it's strictly the man's job to make big decisions, and the wife must follow along. Another person may feel that a big decision should never be made without a full and frank discussion. A third person may feel that a husband and wife have certain areas of autonomy, where they make the decisions without question: the wife pays the bills and buys the furniture, for instance, while the husband decides on what church to attend.

As I have observed marriages, I have seen happy couples making decisions in several different ways. Unhappiness comes when the husband and wife don't agree on the proper process. Sometimes their disagreement develops into a fight, and sometimes it's subtly hidden: the wife, in a classic pattern, may seem to go along with her husband but then manipulates him to get her own way. It's better if you can reach a comfortable agreement about how decisions should be reached.

11. *Do you help each other emotionally?* Everyone gets bruised and discouraged in the course of life. In good marriages both partners draw encouragement and strength from each other. Your partner should be someone you not only admire and have fun with but someone you go to

for healing. He (or she) should have the kind of love that will match your need, that will lift you, restore you, bind your wounds, and help to heal your hurts.

12. *Do you have absolute trust in each other?* Trust has to do with your assessment of a person's character. You trust someone if you have complete confidence that he will do what is right. If you lack trust, nothing can substitute for it. There must be complete trust in your partner's handling of money, drugs, and alcohol. And regarding his (or her) sexual fidelity, confidentiality, treatment of children, Christian faith, work, and truthfulness is essential. A lack of trust in any of these will do more than detract from your happiness. It will completely undermine it. You cannot do without trust.

13. *Are you more creative and energetic because of each other?* Some people say that love makes a person absentminded. It may do that at times. It may also make a person irritable, worried, or depressed—at times. Overall, though, love should give you both more life. Depression, worry, and lethargy are trouble signs. You shouldn't usually get less done because you're in love, but more. Love should make you more determined than ever to make the best of yourself and the work you do because you want your partner to be proud of you, and you feel responsible to him or her. You should bring out the best in each other.

14. *Can you accept and appreciate each other's family?* Most young couples would rather not think about family, especially if the family is unpleasant. When you're young and single you can operate quite independently. However, no man (or woman) is an island. We are part of our families and our families are part of us—whether we like them or not. You don't have to like them, but you do have to accept them because that's essentially the same as accepting your partner. It's best if you can find a way to appreciate them, too. If your relationship depends on excluding the family, it's got a crack in its foundation.

15. *Do you have unresolved relationships in your past?* Love on the rebound is notoriously unstable. You can't make up for something you missed with a previous love—though many people try. You both ought to be able to talk freely about "those who went before." You don't need to talk in detail, but if you just can't talk (or can't stop talking), you may be emotionally stuck in an earlier era. The past needs to be put entirely into the past.

16. *Is sex under control?* If not, it's an unhealthy sign for your future. You'll have to control yourselves many times, in many ways—including sexually—when you're married. If you can't do it now, you may be

unable to do it later. This is not to suggest that you won't have a battle to control sex. The question is, who is winning the battle?

Sex before marriage often masks trouble signs. It provides a false sort of unity, unity based not on commitment but on hormones. Its powerfully attractive force keeps you together and urges you into a false commitment, when without sex your relationship would soon falter. Guilt feelings often accompany premarital sex, adding to the confusion. On the whole, sexual involvement feels good but doesn't help clarify the commitment you want to make. When you've gone "all the way" together—or even most of the way—you may feel you are already essentially married and that a marriage ceremony merely ratifies what you've already done. So you may not think about the commitment as much as you ought to. But the fact is that the marriage ceremony is more than a ceremony. It takes you "all the way" into marriage. Sex doesn't.

17. *Have you spent enough time together?* I don't consider any factor more critical than time. You can't really know each other deeply if you haven't had enough time together. How much is enough? As a rule of thumb, I'd say a year of real closeness is the minimum. In this amount of time you can get beyond the first blinding effects of love and see more clearly what you are committing yourself to.

18. *Have you fought and forgiven?* Walter Trobish, who has written wisely on marriage, said that a couple should summer and winter together. Anybody can get along when the sun is shining. Learning to accept and forgive when you have been hurt requires much more of the stuff that makes happy marriages. In a week of crises you learn more about each other than in a month of happiness. If you cannot forgive, if you hold grudges, if you use "the silent treatment" to get your way, or if disagreement makes you lose your sanity—then you are not ready for marriage. Conflicts will come. You must have a way to overcome them.

19. *Have you talked about each area of your future life?* When you're far along in your relationship and quite serious, you need to systematically discuss your future life. I don't favor doing this on your first date, as some couples do—it should be an activity reserved for the advanced.

Finances, life-style, sexual expectations, jobs, children, and parents are some of the subjects you need to discuss in detail before you're married since you'll be dealing with these things if and when you're married. And you'd better find out beforehand whether you can communicate. A helpful workbook is published by InterVarsity Press, *Handbook for Engaged Couples,* by Bob and Alice Fryling, in which they give you a list of issues to talk over, so you won't overlook anything.

20. *Have you had counseling?* Most couples would rather keep their re-lationship just to themselves—to counsel each other. This kind of priva-cy, while comfortable, ultimately doesn't help. A trained outsider can see you from an angle you yourself can't see. A counselor can't tell you whether marriage is the right move, but he can help you explore ques-tions you've ignored or help solve potential problems. Most pastors ei-ther do marriage counseling themselves or can recommend someone to go to. It's well worth paying for if there's a charge. Usually, if the coun-seling is to be thorough, more than one session is necessary.

IS SEVENTEEN A PASSING SCORE?
While these twenty questions can't be graded like a test, each question is important enough to explain the failure of a marriage. Each one must be considered with great care by both you and your partner as you approach a final decision regarding your future.

On the other hand, you don't have to be perfect or have a perfect rela-tionship to make a happy and fruitful marriage. If marriage required per-fection, all of us would fail. God helps those who ask him for help. He cares for marriage. He helps you make your marriage "the right one."

So what do you do when your wedding day approaches and you aren't sure you're doing the right thing? You should, I believe, treat your doubts as an opportunity to prayerfully think of your partner, perhaps in light of the previous twenty questions. Ask yourself whether you want to make this person the right one for life. Ask yourself whether you can stick to a lifetime with this person—"in sickness and health, for better or worse, for rich or poor."

You should never say "I do" just because you think it's too late to back out. Waiting a little longer is always better than going ahead with a cere-mony you have serious doubts about. As embarrassing and troublesome as it may be, a delay in your plans is not the end of the world. Of course, you have to make a choice at some point, and you will never eliminate all uncertainty. But sometimes extra time can help you be clearer about your choice.

Marriage is too good to enter in the wrong way. The right way is with joy, love, and confidence that you are ready for whatever the future holds with the right one.

The good news for Christians is that they do not have to make this choice alone. God's Spirit helps those who look to him for help, giving them wisdom and discernment in making decisions.

And there is more good news. Our uncertainty does not last indefinitely, as it does for those who do not know God. We do not have to
spend our entire lives wondering if we made the right choice—if the
right one might not be, in fact, some other woman or man. We may suffer through uncertainty, but only for a time. Our wedding day brings joy
partly because we believe we are ending the period of uncertainty and
entering a period of absolute certainty. We have found "the right one."
God himself stamps approval on our marriage. He welcomes us to the
dream.

Q: It seems like lots of people use the term *love* quite loosely. A girl gets
butterflies over a guy and then wonders if she's in love. I have been
brought up with the conception that if you can truly say to someone of the
opposite sex that you love them, that implies a very strong level of commitment. This might be terribly old-fashioned, but it makes sense to me.
Do you feel the term *love* has changed in its use?

A: The word *love* has changed, but perhaps not the way you think. Most of
the Bible's interest is in "agape" love, which is a highly committed, self-
sacrificing love such as that described in 1 Corinthians 13. Yet *love* in the
Bible can reflect a wide variety of meanings. For instance, 2 Samuel 13:1
describes Amnon "falling in love" with Tamar—though his "love" led to
rape.

I don't see any great harm in describing romantic, giddy feelings as
love. How else would we describe them? What concerns me is the temptation to leave love at that level. Love that lasts has, as you say, a very
strong level of commitment.

You may be right to reserve the word *love* for such high levels of commitment. However, I don't see any way to change the way people talk. I'd
rather do this: When someone says, "I love her," I'd ask, "What do you
mean by that?" Love has many meanings, but I know that the best meaning requires far more than a feeling. ▬▬

A couple of years ago I visited a city where I had lived before (here in the U.S.), and I met a guy I'll call Michael. I could tell he was very attracted to me. Even though I thought he was quite likeable, I treated him as just a friend. He had a girlfriend at the time, and I didn't want any problems, especially since his girlfriend and I had been good friends as children.

During my visit he treated me very nicely, and I could tell that he felt really bad about my having to go back to my country. This is where my error (and his) may have been. I told him that I was never coming back to his city because at that time it seemed that way. He seemed pretty sad, and I could tell that he felt sort of upset.

I went back to my country, and about one and a half years later I received word that my childhood friend had married Michael. They had had premarital sex and were forced into a premature marriage. Six months after his wedding (two years after my visit), my family moved back to the same city. The worst part of this is that, by total coincidence, Michael, his wife, and their children moved in right across the street.

Michael has come to my house and talks to my father as a friend. I was able to talk with him alone a couple of times, and he asked me why I had lied to him by telling him that I was never coming back. He told me that things would have been so different. He even said that the only reason he got married was because I didn't show up at his wedding—that if I had, he would have run out of there.

We don't really talk a lot because it's very hard for us. We say hi to each other, and we sometimes talk in front of other family members.

I still care for him, and it's hard for me to see him all the time. I know that nothing can be done about it, besides praying for strength and maybe moving away. I feel so horrible even knowing that I still care for him. I guess I just need some counseling from someone I can trust—you.

A: One form of question has never yet yielded a helpful answer: those that begin, "I wonder what would have happened if . . . ? You might as well spend your hours pretending you're Spider Woman—it's just as realistic!

Most of the anxieties you are feeling stem from "what-if" thinking—*What if I had told him to wait for me? What if he hadn't married her?* There's nothing unusual about feeling attracted to a married man. Your misery comes from the power of your fantasy world—*This guy could have been mine instead of hers!* But that world doesn't exist. It never did and it never will. Its only reality is its power to make you miserable.

A lot of people I hear from fall under that power, suffering because their fantasy world of love doesn't match their lives. Fantasy worlds are hard to dismiss. You can't just turn off your brain—especially when the subject of the fantasy is across the street and thus unavoidable. Moving away would be a good idea, but perhaps it's not practical for you. So I'll mention three things that can help. They're not magical, but if you stick to them they'll change your thinking.

First, be ruthless with your thoughts. Only one world is worth your thoughts—the one you are living in. When you find yourself drifting into self pity and "what-if" thoughts, jerk yourself to attention and remind yourself that that is an imaginary world. Say to yourself, "Grow up!" Don't even let yourself get started on that train of thought. The Apostle Paul tells us in Philippians 4:8 to think about whatever is true, whatever is noble, whatever is right, whatever is pure, and whatever is lovely.

Second, get busy with other things. Make sure you have something else to think about or do, especially when Michael comes around or when you're thinking "what-if" thoughts. Some good friendships would help. Fantasy breeds in a vacuum, especially when you're feeling lonely or bored.

Third, wait. Your strong feelings for Michael are like a thundercloud—solid and threatening in appearance, yet certain to pass and disappear with a change in the weather. Infatuations nearly always have a short life. It may be hard to believe now, but if you can keep clear of Michael and stay busy, his attraction will someday seem ridiculous. To tell you the truth, he sounds somewhere between immature and a jerk. Who does he think he is, talking that way to you? He's married and has a family. ■■

AN AFTERWORD: KEEPING THE DREAM ALIVE

Often, when people think of a Christian approach to sex, they think negatively: "Don't do this," and "Don't do that." Somehow they get the impression that God doesn't approve of sex—that it's an unfortunate necessity you hate to even mention.

That's way off. God is the great idealist. He invented sex for our pleasure. He didn't want us to spend our lives alone. The dream of lifelong love, of endless sexual intimacy, is one that he planted deep in each of our souls.

God is also the great realist. He knows the kind of up-and-down people we are. He knows how hard it is for us to follow through on loving feelings, day after day, month after month, year after year. He knows how prone we are to smash the dream. So he gave a few strict instructions: "Don't do this, or you'll hurt yourself. Don't do that, or you'll misuse my great invention." The rules he gave are often negative, but they're based on something extremely positive: the making or restoring of the dream.

It's astonishing. God, the Maker of the universe, cares about our sexual fulfillment. He is not content to have us wander through life managing occasional glimpses of happiness. He wants us to live in sexual splendor, with one love so strong it never dies. And he makes it possible for us to live the dream. It isn't automatic. It's never easy. But it *is* possible.

For fifteen years I've been answering questions about sex, hearing from every kind of person with every question imaginable. Often the problems they present seem overwhelming, and I have to wonder—is there any hope?

Yet in my own life, and in the life of friends and family, I've seen God's wisdom confirmed. My marriage isn't just like I dreamed it might be when I was thirteen. It's better, richer, more fulfilling, more fun. Also, it's terrifically challenging. It takes all I have to give and pays back dividends in return.

That reality, lived day by day, helps me as I answer difficult questions. Many people are in the dark when it comes to sexual satisfaction, and it's hard for them to imagine how bright the light can be. It's hard for them to be patient and hopeful and disciplined when all they see is darkness. One of my jobs is to shine around a little of the light.

So I say: the dream can come true. Don't let it die.

CAMPUS LIFE is the largest, most colorful Christian youth magazine in the world. Month after month, CAMPUS LIFE helps thousands of teens keep their faith intact in a world falling apart. Like a trusted friend, it provides solid counsel, encouragement and just plain fun.

☐ Please send me a full year (10 issues) of CAMPUS LIFE for only $11.95—40% off the cover price.

☐ Payment enclosed
☐ Please bill me

Name _____

Address _____

City _____ State ___ Zip _____

Please allow 4-6 weeks for delivery of first issue.
Outside U.S.: add $3/year for delivery.
(U.S. FUNDS ONLY)

Do you need answers on other tough issues?

Loneliness
Family
Fear
Sex
Self-image
Death
Friendship

E8CCLBKN

CAMPUS LIFE is the largest, most colorful Christian youth magazine in the world. Month after month, CAMPUS LIFE helps thousands of teens keep their faith intact in a world falling apart. Like a trusted friend, it provides solid counsel, encouragement and just plain fun.

☐ Please send me a full year (10 issues) of CAMPUS LIFE for only $11.95—40% off the cover price.

☐ Payment enclosed
☐ Please bill me

Name _____

Address _____

City _____ State ___ Zip _____

Please allow 4-6 weeks for delivery of first issue.
Outside U.S.: add $3/year for delivery.
(U.S. FUNDS ONLY)

Do you need answers on other tough issues?

Loneliness
Family
Fear
Sex
Self-image
Death
Friendship

E8CCLBKN

NO POSTAGE
NECESSARY
IF MAILED
IN THE
UNITED STATES

BUSINESS REPLY MAIL

FIRST CLASS   PERMIT NO. 1596   WHEATON, IL

POSTAGE WILL BE PAID BY ADDRESSEE

CAMPUS LIFE
Subscription Services
P.O. Box 8012
Wheaton, IL 60189-9812

NO POSTAGE
NECESSARY
IF MAILED
IN THE
UNITED STATES

BUSINESS REPLY MAIL

FIRST CLASS   PERMIT NO. 1596   WHEATON, IL

POSTAGE WILL BE PAID BY ADDRESSEE

CAMPUS LIFE
Subscription Services
P.O. Box 8012
Wheaton, IL 60189-9812